Dedicated...

to those who believe in limitless possibilities, and so move

forward a step at a time, day after day and year after

year...

Creating

Change

Contents

Winners

Poetry

1st place
Allan Johnston's "Hard"

2nd place: Alison Luterman's "Voice of the Turtle"

3rd place: Susan Baller-Shepard's "Pangaea"

Lylanne Musselman's "Perfectionist"

Prose

1st place
M. Garrett Bauman's "Skin"

2nd place: Jill Koenigsdorf's "Life and Death in the Backyard"

3rd place: Pamela Balluck's "Images 'Only'"

Bill Sherwonit's "Back on the Hillside…"

Entries: Images "Only"
Pamela Balluck

8/12. From my lounge chair, nested in the wild lawn—Perseids, a tidepool of meteors like minnows, swarms of spermatozoids, spermatozoa set free. There. There. Gone.

Imagine: Adam climbing Mount Anchises with her birthday cake, with earrings he forged from siderites, like sparks.

✵

8/26. Outlaw Inn, on my own for Chuck Florence Quartet. Bass-fiddle player dances with, sings to, woos, his instrument—she's taller than he is.

✵

8/29. Neighbor raking gravel back into her offshoot from the oxbow of our drive: two tracks disappear.

✵

9/12. First night of life-drawing. My instructor has puffy, swollen bags under his eyes, like mine from Adam-grief.

✵

9/13. Rocks smash into my windshield—as if every day on this cut-off road, someone snipes at me.

✵

9/19. Last night I dreamed my steering wheel cracked, split (like a hoop earring).

✵

9/24. Silver says in a letter-tape from Colorado: "Seems like every time you get to riding on this crest of love and enthusiasm, he begins to sink away from you."

※

9/29. Fall colors are competing with the fresh double-gold line up the blacktop highway.

※

10/3. Dream I had last night: Was with Adam and his youngest, Ky. We found an old door. I took a bite of out it, redwood or cedar.

※

10/12. Blue clouds near sunset—turn to lavender.

※

Tuesday p.m. Adam's car at the community college—close up, unlike the similar Subarus that mistakenly send adrenaline rushing, on highways, in town, on our road: tow hitch on rear, sweetgrass on dash. I park next to him.

※

10/27. I dreamed seeing through my window the trees flocked with snow.

※

Tuesday p.m. Halloween.
     Adam's car again at the college—flatbed-trailer hitched—parked perpendicular to slots; rusted lines of pipe; long sheets of stainless. He made another pick-up in Seattle. I wonder if he saw her. Soon will be a newborn sculpture standing in his field.
     On my way out of town, I buy some smoke.
     In my rearview, on my way home, a car with one headlight brighter than the other; I allow it to pass.
     Coming toward me, car with left headlight only. In my rearview, one tail light only.
     Coming toward me—car with right headlight only.

Half-moon is bright—shows off the snow-covered Bluegills at night.

❋

11/8. White gulls against grey sky over white pastures.

❋

11/9. After last night's rain, clumps of snow appear to be Styrofoam cups in the roadside grass.

❋

11/13. Fresh-turned fields, dusted with snow, are pans of unsliced brownies powdered with sugar.

❋

11/16. The tree outside my window, now that leaves are gone, reminds me of the tree reaching up as it reaches down in the Fogel poem tacked to my wall, "Beholden." The tree's branches look like perfect roots—like Buddhist trees, which appear normal upside-down.

❋

11/25. Imprinted into the muddy trail along the New River Road, tracks of dogs, birds, horses, deer, two-wheelers, me.

❋

12/8.   Prose: Birds fly in the shape of a bird flying.

   Poem:

   Birds fly
   in the shape of a
   bird flying.

❋

12/16. On the moonscaped Old River Road, potholes appear corona'd by—rimmed with—shattered glass.

✺

12/19. Just as I notice the snow falling, the sun rising, a bird song. Friday, first day of winter.

✺

12/31 (from Adam's picture window). Two dogs, a German Shepherd and a small black-and-white, cross the melting ice of the Gash River to explore the woodland on the other side. Lucky dogs walk on water. They make it there and back.

Two flickers, black-triangle-chested, red under wings, on the old birch tree.

Two magpies are cavorting.

✺

1/19. Outside my window, a sky of cotton batting heads east, across the Rockies.

✺

2/1. Weather has warmed, so that the neighbor's corral is a lake, and horses stand pissed off on islands.

✺

3/16. The rhythmic sound that comes to my ears like a handsaw from across the river appears to be a raven passing over—the sounds of its wings intensified by a stick clutched in beak, about the same length as—width of—its wingspan.

✺

4/3. Neighbor goes out to check on his cattle (they are calving); finds a cow (who calved three days ago) dead, her bag cut off, female organs removed, a small cylindrical chunk cut from her flank. There's no blood anywhere—none in her, none on her, none around her. We cannot find the calf.

4/26. What sounds, from my house, like a car approaching is really the wind driving through woods between my place and Adam's.

5/11. An eyelash is a parenthesis
(at the beginning of an ink-jetted line.

5/24. Fat robin red breast at trail's edge; I almost kick it. Alive, standing on both legs, feet firmly planted side by side.
   I am indecisive out of ignorance.
   Its eyes open only when I unsquat and decide to move on.

6/2. Robin red breast at trail's edge. It's dead. Looks like a horse kicked it.
   I talk to Adam about what I could have/should have done and he says maybe the best or most would have been to move the bird gently to another place, where it might have died in peace or mended.

6/3. The bug smashed on my printed page leaves blood smeared from one double-spaced line to the next—the red already rusting.

6/8. On the Old River Road, I come upon the shiny, flat squiggles of run-over snakes.

7/15. I gently move myself to another place.

Skin

M. Garrett Bauman

I uncovered the translucent, twisted snakeskin in my woodpile. The outside layer was scaled, crumbly, and split lengthwise, while the inner layer was elastic and ribbed with bony hoops. Sometime the previous summer when we were shedding our own old lives, the snake had slithered into a crevice among the logs to crawl out of itself.

The shedding of skin should be a private act, but Carol's and my shedding had been a public flaying. Town criers were sent to the far corners of the kingdom with news, rumors, myths and lies. We supposedly left our children home alone while we rendezvoused. We supposedly participated in "orgies" to slake feverish sexual appetites. The truth—that we rarely saw each other and loved each other deeply and spiritually—was far more terrifying than orgies and child neglect. People need to divide the world into saints and satyrs.

The outer layer of our lives was ripped away by parents, lawyers, townspeople, bankers and real estate agents, who felt as free to pry into our financial dealings, child visitations and living arrangements as if they investigated a terrorist cell. Although I had never bounced a check, people now demanded pre-payment or cash. Functionaries demanded to know who paid what bills and how long my children would live with me each year. You don't realize how naked you can be until someone in your small town cranes her neck as you pass and then hurriedly whispers to her elderly companion. Or until you hear gossip about you come home through your children. Not only small town folk are susceptible. A professor in my department burst into my office one day to announce that my divorce inflicted intense headaches on her. She glared, expecting an apology.

"What do you think it's doing to me?" I said testily. She didn't speak to me for months.

Carol and I had friends who cared about us, who worried about the exhaustion in our eyes and weight loss. So much of us that was normally shadowy and safe lay spread eagled in the town square. But few people sensed that we were shedding a deeper elastic layer of our lives as well— the secret skin of our inner life. I'd wake up in the morning with Carol leaning over me. She laughed. "I understand you, but I don't know if I'd recognize you in a crowd." We studied each square inch of the other's skin and found wonderful, strange things the owner never noticed. I stroked Carol's bare back with a forefinger, learning the contours of each muscle and her spine's knucklings. I studied freckles, pores and markings, peering closer, then closer still, each dot a star, and tinier ones receding in the distance until her skin was no longer a flat map but as deep as space. I didn't stare at it so much as into it.

We explored what hid under our skins too, to help the new creatures out. We heard music differently through the other's ears. Painters and novelists helped scratch off our old skins. We studied the world's six great religions in detail, searching each for its truth, putting aside what we thought previously and what we were supposed to think. We accepted no "givens," believed that with the other's help, all our skins could be peeled away or outgrown. We dragged our pasts from the closets of memory. Religion, politics, family holidays, meals, books, schools. We needed to rebuild the years we did not have each other.

In the house I uncoiled the snakeskin on my desk amid the clutter of an oriole's nest, a cicada's discarded skin, a striped fungus and a dozen other relics. Many had been given to me by students to verify what they had seen. I have a mantra for my classes: "We are what we see. What is invisible to us defines our limitations and prejudices."

I needed to follow my own advice. I had barely begun to dig into the few square feet of real estate I lived in. I twirled the snakeskin in my fingers and tested its elasticity. You should stretch out of your skin each season of your life. Like most people, I had not finished all my youth's work. But as I crawled toward middle age, I needed to wriggle out of the dead skin of my twenties and thirties and leave it behind so whatever new creature was in me might crawl free.

When I watched my excited students fan through our woods and field, it was hard to believe I was the teacher. Too often I gave them nothing but superficial facts, the dead skins of knowledge. "Thou shouldst not have been old till thou hadst been wise," the Fool counsels Lear. Amen. But when did I become a "professor" and not just someone who liked to read and write and walk in the woods? When did the tender, awkward amateur disappear? The one who was still on the same side of thirty with them, the one who didn't realize how little time we have to learn the things that matter? I never noticed him peeling off. And when the final integument is unzipped at the end of life, will I finally be wise then, or will I shed all my layers only to find I was nothing but skin?

Once at my desk I swatted a threatening wasp and cleanly severed its head with the blow. The headless body walked back and forth on my desk for two days. It was calm, unperturbed, as though adjusting to life in a more peaceful dimension. I studied it with terrified fascination. The border between life and death seemed less defined than I wanted it to be. Was a life without thinking or intent possible? Who would want it? The wasp's wings whirred occasionally, not for take-off, but as if flexing inactive muscles. Its stinger pulsed more placidly too, not the way a mind-troubled wasp's does—like an itchy trigger. In its travels the wasp stumbled into its own severed head, which somehow became stuck to the underside of its thorax. It felt the head occasionally with its front legs as though inquiring what it was, then continued its stroll with the head slung under it like a basket, the eyes staring out backwards between its rear legs to see where it had been. It was a metaphor for how we live much of the time. When death glazes my eyes, I might finally be able to say, "Ah, that was what my life was!"

A teacher is a professional slougher of skins—a disillusioner and re-creator. My students wanted to see Animal Planet scenes—otters frolicking, eagles mating or wolves dragging down a deer. But groups of people make too much noise, have too little time or patience. I told them to start small, for there are guaranteed secrets everywhere. "Look in a square foot of soil," I advised. "Scrape aside leaves, poke into stumps, roll over rotting logs." I wanted them to realize that mystery and adventure were everywhere, and they complied, but often felt let down finding only bugs. Sometimes, though, while doing little things, a secret crawled up one's boot, as a ten-inch black, yellow-spotted salamander did to a student quietly sifting through leaves. Once, two students were down in a creek bed studying a bird's mud nest when a twelve-point buck thrashed through a thicket and bounded over their heads. Another time watching newts in a shallow pool, several students and I chillingly became aware of the shape of a snapping turtle buried in the ooze under water. What had seemed folded leaves focused into a pointed beak and carapace. It made me wonder what else watched us and what secrets were invisible in plain view.

I have always been a spy on life, always peeked behind the curtains and walls that skinned me in. At East Side High School across the street from my Paterson house, any scrap of bushes could be the scene of a couple's after-school tryst I could observe. I picked up new curses on Saturday nights eavesdropping on the plate-throwing spats at the Rollins house when the daughter stumbled in drunk. The house on the other side had a gap in the curtains that sometimes allowed a peek at Mrs. Tdeski drying off after her shower. I checked in pretty often. Once Mrs. T's elderly mother was there instead—also naked. I was revolted and disgusted at myself, but could not tear my eyes away from her pachyderm skin. Here was Mrs. T. fifty years in the future, and I realized that time would tell its secrets to those who looked, that all skins will be stripped in season.

As a boy I thrived on costumes—new skin for each day. I had a cowboy outfit and Dad's old army hats and jacket. I was Davy Crockett, Baron Von Richthofen, or Robin Hood. Even death was just another costume. I spent hours perfecting being shot and killed. I caught mortar shells, machine gun bullets and knives and fell through hedges and down stairs.

"Stop falling down the stairs!" Mom would yell. "You'll break your neck!"

"What the hell is the matter with him?" my father groaned.

I didn't care. I gasped, choked, said last words, crumpled, tumbled or flopped to the floor, heaved in final convulsions, then arose and experimented with a new way to die. There were plenty of lives, deaths and rebirths out there.

I wanted to become something but what? Something more than just old. Even when I could label myself as graduate student, husband, father, teacher, I still felt like someone else's idea of me.

After splitting apart our old lives, Carol and I had to grow new skin. "Skin for two" might be my best definition of a good marriage. We shed spouses, parents, and some friends, as well as a healthy percentage of our dignity, social inhibitions, obedience and blind beliefs. Our possessions had been decimated. Yet we found ourselves freer the more was taken away, and soon willingly purged our lives. As each bag of stuff left the house, as each desiccated relationship or idea was abandoned, our shape became more sharply defined.

During this fall semester's nature expedition, a young woman student asked me about the galls on goldenrod, those brown, golf-ball size lumps that swelled from the plants' stems. I explained that they grow where a wasp punctures the stalk and lays an egg when the stem is young and tender. After the egg hatches, the wasp larva secretes a growth-stimulating chemical that induces the plant to produce a node of soft cells for the larva to eat. Another larval chemical makes the plant's stem-support cells multiply cancerously into plump insulation to protect the developing wasp. The gall is essentially a layer of thick skin around the larva—skin for two, although not the kind a good marriage has.

After my explanation, the student wanted to know how big the larva was, if it were dormant, if it were wasp or larva at the moment. "I don't know," I told her. "Find out."

She commandeered a penknife, peeled away the dead, brown crust, and cut wedges from the spongy, white gall. Inside was a yellow-white grub less than half an inch long. Its own thin skin barely contained its gelatinous insides. It had been relying on the gall to keep its insides in. Was it metamorphosing into wings and stinger as we watched? My students glanced at me; they wanted to trust their teacher, yet doubted that this blob would transform into a hard-shelled, aggressive flying machine. I knew it could happen, knew the possibilities of change were far more eerie and profound than most people suspected, knew the thing we come from might not resemble what we become.

Someone prodded the larva with a stem of straw. It rippled like a tiny waterbed. "What's going to happen to this one now?" he asked.

"It's going to die," I said.

"Couldn't we put it back?" asked the woman who had performed the surgery. I didn't answer. She returned the penknife, shifted the dissected gall with its exposed larva from hand to hand. I took it from her the way a professor can, so it seems as if there were a scientific use for it. She felt she had become a killer. Blind to my own changes, as snakes are during sloughing when they lose the eye scale that serves as a focal lens, I could see her changes with clarity, pride and pity.

"There are many more," I said, nodding toward the patch of goldenrod bending in the October wind.

That was no answer, of course, but it was the only comfort I had to offer. We say nature is "satisfied" by the survival of species, that individual deaths do not matter; yet nature endures the creation and extinction of millions of species with no sign of satisfaction or dissatisfaction. But if individuals don't matter, why all these elaborate transformations from one form to another, why all these skins to house nothing? If we live for our children and they live for theirs, who will really live?

The universe itself has a skin—somewhere out there—18 billion light years away where the original remnants of the cosmic big bang still hurtle outward in all directions. That skin is utterly naked. The universe grows at a rate near the speed of light, pushing its thin layer of radiation and dust into the nothing. This elastic skin contains us all. Outside it lies nothingness beyond human comprehension, and inside that membrane of existence, 99.999…percent is vacuum. It is like us—a bit of skin stretched over the emptiness. For a long moment the class watched the patch of goldenrod tilt and spring back in a capricious breeze. Other larvae were safely chewing inside their spongy galls in the October sun, but we felt the coming snow hissing among the stems. A sunny May morning would stir the wasp larvae to complete their changes and gnaw out, spreading wet wings to dry as they clung to the outside of the dead galls that nourished them. Perhaps next spring someone would wander among them to spy on the holes in the galls from which life escaped, perhaps slitting galls that had no holes to see if the creature inside had withered, incapable of the great change required. Can a snake or human suffocate because it refuses to make the effort to shed? I don't understand how that could be, but I wonder. Deep in our own resilient layers, working our own changes, none of us knew what we would be then, when it was time to come back to look.

22

The Woman with Dragonfly Earrings
Marcella Darin

Some Native American cultures regard the dragonfly as a symbol of renewal after hardship. Now, still as a dragonfly hovering over a lily pad, she ponders this among other symbols she's learning about. In a few minutes she will have to get the girls. Melting deeper into her favorite yoga pose affectionately known as the corpse, she lies on her back and stretches her legs, palms upward toward a tottering ceiling fan. Her mind is lulled into neutral by the "ayummm" of her neighbor's air conditioner. Mark's left for work before sunrise; his down pillow is creased with his imprint.

The digital clock reads 8:10. She bargains with herself. If she skips toasting her bagel, she can stay a couple more minutes. Breathing deeply, she watches her belly poof up under her sleep shirt. Relax, she tells herself. A few months ago, she had asked her therapist how to become more courageous.

"It's like riding a bike," was her response. "You just have to practice, Rachel." She has a flashback of her mother in a darkened bedroom praying to St. Jude. If you had lost your job or were fighting cancer, this saint was the go-to guy, the one to entrust with a Mission Impossible. One time the novena actually worked, and her dad found a job teaching chemistry at the high school.

Rachel recites the few words she remembers of the never-fail novena prayer, imploring the good St. Jude to "bring visible and speedy help." It couldn't hurt to summon the sacred artillery, she reasons.

Suddenly Annie and Sylvie appear at the bedroom door. They are holding cereal bowls, their spoons diving for Fruit Loops on the milky surface. Rachel tells them to get their school clothes from the laundry basket. The first top Annie picks out—her favorite with the Monkey face—fits her like a second skin, so Rachel makes her daughter go back and choose something else. In a few years, she thinks, this may be a battle she has to surrender. She shepherds her daughters downstairs and shoos them out the front door.

Back upstairs she slips into the silky black dress she carefully selected the night before. Lovingly she fingers the black lacquered box that holds her earrings. Her favorites are the peacock feathers Annie gave her for her birthday last year; glittery dragonflies for the beach; and teardrop turquoise earrings which she chooses.

She is a little overdressed for her office's "Casual Thursday," but the outfit makes her feel good. Confident. She reminds herself that she can be tough underneath her baby face exterior. She had held her dying father's hand in the ICU ward when the ventilator was unplugged. She had pushed two babies into this world—didn't even need a Tylenol. She had wheeled her turban-headed mom around the nursing home, deftly avoiding parked wheelchairs to arrive first in the dining hall. And she can do this.

She catches her usual 10:30 a.m. Metro train and pulls a book of Zen meditations from her canvas tote, hoping its wisdom will calm her soul. Her day is filled with departmental meetings about the power point presentation she is drafting for a new client. She knows to sprinkle her copy with key words that demonstrate her mastery of the marketing plan for a new charter school. Using terms such as "Integrated communication"..."selling the brand"..."interactive web design," she is at the top of her game. The busyness is a useful diversion from the encounter with Mark she faces this evening. She munches on a few Saltine crackers for lunch.

When she arrives home from the office, she arranges for Sylvie and Annie to stay at a friend's house and coolly tells Mark they have an appointment with a rental agent. He won't suspect anything since their lease expires next month. Before following Mark to their station wagon, she drops to her knees on the kitchen floor still sticky with cereal and whispers a prayer to the no-fail St. Jude. And then she takes a couple deep breaths.

She straps on her seat belt and makes a mental list of every horrible, hateful thing that Mark has ever done. In a novel she admires, the protagonist screws up her courage this way. Her mind conjures visions of Mark's cruelty, shuddering as she relives his violent tantrums: when Sylvie had strep, a fever of 104 degrees and needed to go to the doctor, Mark "needed" to relieve his own stress, stormed out to their Ford Taurus and drove it to Oak Street beach, leaving Rachel and Sylvie to take a taxi; when she asked him to read "Good Night, Moon" to Annie, he slapped Rachel's face and ripped the book to shreds in a sudden eruption of rage; when her mother sat alone that first night, newly grieving her only sister's death from a car crash in far away Vancouver, Mark refused to watch their girls so Rachel could console her mom. He went to the Pioneer Tap instead, coming home drunk and waking Sylvie and Annie with his screaming. That was the worst. Some things are unforgivable.

By the time Rachel reaches her destination, her palms are soaked with sweat and her heart is racing as if she's run a half-marathon. An early summer blackout has left her lawyer's neighborhood dark and silent. She remembers the first time she met with Kristine; that same afternoon she had a call from the temp agency offering her a job with a marketing firm. She took this as a sign: that when you do the right thing for the right reason, the universe will propel you forward like a water slide swooshes you into a pool.

She and Mark are now seated around Kristine's mahogany table. As Rachel gives him the divorce papers, Mark's jaw drops so low his bearded chin nearly grazes the table. He skims the first page by candlelight. His hazel eyes, accusing her of betrayal, burn as bright as the candles' flames. Rachel tells him that she and the girls are moving out at month's end— without him. When it is over, Mark calls a taxi to go to a motel. Rachel returns to their apartment solo.

The next morning, Rachel wakes up with the giddiness of a ten-year-old packing for a dream vacation at Disney World. She takes several garbage bags from the pantry, stuffs them with Mark's clothes, and sets them in the hallway outside the apartment door. She gets blonde streaks in her hair and buys herself pink carnations along with the week's groceries. She gets a call from her friend Liz where Annie and Sylvie have spent the night. Time to get the girls. She feels like blaring her horn, trumpeting to a sleepy Saturday world that she has finally done it. If she never, ever does anything else of value, at least she's done this one thing.

Her therapist has said when Tina left Ike, she only had a nickel in her purse. You just do what you must do—sounds so simple.

On their first night in the new apartment Annie sobs as she carries boxes of clothes up two flights of stairs to a vintage apartment with tons of space, but with few amenities like multiple electric outlets in the same room. In the bedroom where four-year-old Sylvie refuses to sleep, someone has scrawled, "Help," on the wall in red crayon. Rachel notices darkening clouds outside the bedroom window.

Sylvie and Annie huddle on the sofa, surrounded by leaning towers of half-empty cardboard boxes. Rachel holds her daughters, telling them the old Chinese proverb that what does not kill them would make them stronger. As she finishes her sentence, a violent thunderclap shakes the apartment building.

The summer is steamy. If Rachel could wring the sky, it would fill a few dozen swimming pools in well-heeled Wilmette, where Mark grew up. Or at least where he had made a feeble attempt. In between work and taking care of her girls, Rachel feathers their third-floor nest. Eager to discover treasures for their new home, she haunts garage sales and finds a small oak desk for the girls and an old cigar chest that can double as a coffee table. She becomes a quarter-hoarder, stashing away coins for the laundry. She has secrets that make her feel competent. She's learned that the washer on the right needs only two quarters; that a plunger is better and cheaper than a plumber; that she can assemble a new Hoover, then triumphantly watch it suck Cheerios off the living room floor.

There are times when she thinks she should be somewhere else by now, cozy in a bungalow with tomatoes to plant and sump pumps and leaky furnaces to worry about. After the street lights click on, after she washes the dishes, signs trip permission slips and folds towels, she drifts into sleep mode with her PC.

Rachel doesn't feel alone, just crazy overwhelmed. Somehow nights are easier—the soft buzz from the traffic on Harlem Avenue soothes her. Even the wail of sirens reminds her that she is not a lone soul. For the first time in 20 years, there is room for her small library of French novels on her shelf: Proust and Zola, Sartre and Camus join books on mindfulness by Jon Kabat-Zinn.

On a warm September evening, she stands with her girls at the curb holding lit white candles, lifting them like vigil lights to cars speeding by on Harlem Avenue. Annie gets excited whenever a car honks and waves madly. It has been just three days since terrorists reduced the World Trade Center to piles of twisted metal and tears.

Rachel turns at the sound of a basketball being dribbled on the sidewalk. She recognizes George, who recently moved in with his grandmother in the apartment below theirs. In a raspy "don't mess with me" tone, Arlene tells her grandson to set the ball down and join Rachel's family at the curb. "Now, mister," she orders, waving a red candle in a glass jar from last Christmas. Annie, who has a secret crush on George, leans over to light her classmate's candle. George responds with shy smile.

Arlene sidesteps toward Rachel to make room for the couple that lives across from her: Ernie, a Viet Nam vet and his girlfriend, Janice. Ernie carries a shoe-boxed size American flag; Janice has a pillar candle that hints of patchouli. In one smooth move, Ernie takes a matchbook out of his shirt pocket and lights Janice's candle. There is a little flicker as a gust of wind takes them by surprise, but the flame holds steady and true. Janice clears her throat and speaks. "We saw you down here from our kitchen window, and thought it would a good thing to join you all," she tells the small cluster of neighbors.

Rachel notices an older couple cross the street toward them. Despite the mild night, the woman has a black shawl draped over her shoulders. Rachel recognizes them as the couple that operates the flower shop across the street. The older woman is carrying a bouquet of tea roses—the palest yellow tinged with orange—the color of dawn. Reaching the curb, the older woman gives each neighbor three blooms. "A tea rose means you will never forget," she whispers. "We wanted to, to..." And then she cannot speak.

Her husband jumps in to finish her sentence, as people do who have lived together a long time. "What Rosa is trying say is that we want to thank you for remembering." He catches Rachel's questioning gaze. "Our son, Bernard, worked at the Aonq Corporation in the second tower."

The couple, both weeping now, joins the tiny row of vigil keepers. Rachel puts her arm around Rosa, pulling her close enough to notice her Wind Song perfume. They decide to meet tomorrow for cider and doughnuts at the Saturday town market.

The next Wednesday, on the eve of her 20th wedding anniversary, she vows to try something her yoga teacher would say pushed her boundaries. After checking out the "Misc." section of the Daily Journal, she settles on a folk dance group meeting in the basement of a nearby Methodist church. Soon she is whirling across the linoleum floor, grateful for the dizziness that blurs her grief. Not that she is sorry for her broken marriage. No, never that. Instead, she grieves for the lost years it took her to break free. She drinks lukewarm tea from a Styrofoam cup, biting her lip to stop her eyes from tearing. Her awkwardness is as thick as a muggy August afternoon at the zoo. A gangly man in overalls who resembles Garrison Keillor drags a folding chair next to hers and sits down. He tells her how he met his wife of 50 years at a dance marathon in Milwaukee. "That's why we started this group here," he says. "It's the dance that's kept us together."

She listens politely, nodding at all the right places. Suddenly she hears music she recognizes from Zorba the Greek. The storyteller's face lights up in a smile and he bounds to his feet, extending a hand toward Rachel. "Come, try it," he gently implores. "It's the grapevine." She glances at the growing circle of dancers and shakes her head. It's late, she explains, and she must let her sitter go home—tomorrow is a school day.

She pays the sitter, a niece of Rosa's, and the girl flashes her a brilliant smile, glad for the early send-off. Rachel tiptoes into her daughters'

bedroom and plants a kiss on foreheads smelling like Dove soap. When she kisses Sylvie's cheek, her daughter kisses back into the air.

In her own bedroom Rachel pulls out a green, leather-bound journal she has hidden in her drawer beneath the black negligee she's stopped wearing years ago. She reads aloud an entry from June: "For some of us survivor types, leaving is in the gray zone. There are no black eyes or empty Scotch bottles or half-used matchbooks from a downtown hotel. We are the only witnesses to our emotional battering, something which makes our choice to leave even more agonizing in its solitude. Still, there is more choice than we think we have."

Choice. So true. She turns to read the message on a scribbled yellow post-it stuck to her computer screen. "It is never too late to become the person you always wanted to be"—words of wisdom from a woman who wore trousers and used a man's name to be taken seriously. "Thank you, George Sands," she whispers. Rachel, proud wearer of dragonfly earrings, touches one of the glittery winged creatures as she moves to the open window. A star above catches her eye. Or is it a star? Have clouds momentarily obscured it, or is it a blinking light—a jet full of passengers hoping to land safely at O'Hare?

Chokecherries
Donna J. Emerson

We walked, twelve cousins across this road.
Up from the barn to the house.
An arm-in-arm phalange, drinking sun,
summer feet in dirt, heads in clouds.
We felt each others' ribs.

We thought the gathering storm in the trees
swept us forward, toward our families.
Certain in that wind, buffeted by those maples
planted on our land. Mothers laughing on the lawn.

Fifty summers passed.
The farmhouse burned one July when we
weren't there.
We were growing, moving to new states.
One by one, our mothers died.
The barn caved in last April's late snow,
splayed upon itself. The hay loft remains
with the same hay we pitched there.

Karen's ex-husband John owns her land now.
He bought her out. He likes to kill deer,
with a bow, says he'll burn the barn.
We take some hemlock to make a shed.
We walk in fours, now,

alliances broken, mothers scattered in earth.
A storm lights the sky, makes us jump,
shivering trees. Nature takes back the land.
We see a black bear running from
the glade of chokecherries.

In the Glen
Matt Forrest Esenwine

Old stump
rotting, torn by time, shredded with age
browned and blackened through fires and storms,
impassioned hooves and finely-honed axes.

Long ago, abandoned even by ants and mites and worms
who took what they could, consumed their fill
and, satiated and exhausted,
left
to scavenge elsewhere.

Rings once worn proudly
perfect, circumscribe –
nearly inscrutable
like the history they keep.
In younger years
its boughs bore fruit;
lush canopy, shade;
firewood,
home,
a vessel.

Now
as old stump dies
softly
bark and pith and fiber fall away to compost
and one lone leaf – green, young, hopeful –
sprouts forth from the remains...

Birds of Paradise
Catherine Underhill Fitzpatrick

New York Fashion Week is a world apart. Intrinsically material, it spins off into the surreal without a backward glance, a dawn-to-dawn ode to the glorification of the human form presented on blank-eyed starvelings. It is louche and haute, sinful and sublime.

Each spring and fall, more than a hundred American designers roll out their upcoming collections on runways scattered like Pick Up Sticks across the city's five boroughs. On hand to document the shows are legions of fashion writers, editors and photographers. From 1997 to 2003, I covered the action on and off the Fashion Week runways for the *Milwaukee Journal Sentinel.* Did so, in fact, gladly.

Forty years ago, fashion shows were decorous little gatherings where store buyers and esteemed customers perched on white bamboo chairs and watched a stately parade of models walk about the room, elbows crooked at sharp angles. By the late 1990s, decorum was passé. PETA activists tossed a bucket of red paint onto a Randolph Duke runway. Donna Karan sent bare-breasted models out in skirts that resembled Hefty Cinch Saks. And uniformed police quelled a raucous crowd outside a star-studded P Diddy show. Today, 13-year-old fashion bloggers have muscled their way into Fashion Week. They slouch in the front row, projecting an air of entitled complacency while peering into tiny luminescent screens and opining with swift, darting thumbs.

For a long while, though, the hub of Fashion Week was Bryant Park, a pocket-sized greensward dotted with mottle-bark sycamores and extemporaneous groupings of French folding chairs. It was a short walk from my hotel to the park, where runway shows were scheduled on the hour. Each morning I made my way to the park's Sixth Avenue approach and joined a throng of fashionable ticket-holders milling about, assessing one another with practiced up-down glances. At some imperceptible signal, we filed into the maw of a great white tent and, like cows urged along a chute, and shuffled through velvet rope switchbacks to one of three smaller show tents.

Groping for purchase in the dark, I'd stumble along metal risers flanking the runway and somehow find the section, row, and seat scrawled on the back of my ticket. I knew roughly where to go, for Fashion Week seating charts mirror a stringent hierarchy in which one's status is clear, public, and immutable. Students from Parsons and the Fashion Institute of Technology were the lowest of the low, banished to the tents' dreary heights. Lacking a view of the runway or a run-of-show, they were left to glean the trends empirically. Those of middling importance — reporters from medium-sized newspapers in medium-sized cities, such as Milwaukee — were relegated to the vast middle rungs. Celebrities were enthroned in the front row, their choreographed arrivals accompanied by a firestorm of camera strobes and a love-fest of air kisses.

During the wait for a show to begin, my reporter friends and I would chat over the low thump of techno-music heavy on the bass and try to identify incoming celebrities, a challenge we dealt with collaboratively.

"Who's that? Is it somebody?"

"BeBe Neuwirth."

"Nah. Julie Louis-Dreyfuss."

"Sofia Coppola was at Marc Jacobs last night. Wait, is that Hilary Swank down there?"

"Where? What's she wearing?"

"I got Ethan Hawke two chairs from Sofia. God, what's with the forever bed hair?"

"Is Hawke with an 'e'?"

Time is a stretchy thing at Fashion Week. There are two seasons, not four, and they are perpetually six months ahead of themselves. Spring is celebrated the previous fall. Fall is observed the previous spring. Pastels appear in September. Tweeds go on display in March. Fashion week isn't a week, either. It's eight days. Sometimes nine. And ten o'clock in the evening never means ten o'clock. It means at midnight, or thereabouts.

Waiting for a show to begin was particularly nettlesome if there were no certifiable stars twinkling in the front row. When that happened, reporters elevated most anyone to celebrity status. Kimora Lee Simmons. Kathie Lee Gifford. One of the fabulous Miller sisters. We knew them all. Pia Miller (married a Getty). Alexandra Miller (snagged a von Furstenberg). Or Marie-Chantal (Greek prince). In the worst case scenario, we recorded the news that *Vogue* editor Anna Wintour was seen wearing fur and sun glasses, again.

When the stage crew finally amped up the music, took the tent to black, and lashed the runway with laser flashes, the lead model would glide out, clomp to the end of the runway and back and disappear, trailed at close range by clones wearing slightly different ensembles.

Seventeen minutes. From Carolina Herrera to Oscar de la Renta, from Betsey Johnson to Badgley Mischka to Yeohlee to Marc Jacobs to

Proenza Schouler, eighty or ninety unwearable and unaffordable outfits would rocket around a runway in seventeen minutes, give or take a last Hefty Sak skirt. At $100,000 and up, the cost of putting on a show drove some young designers out of business. But exposure is the currency of Fashion Week, and the payback for a successful show—a nod from *Women's Wear Daily*, a glowing report in *Elle*, or a photo in *InStyle*—was enough to launch a new design house into the stratosphere.

At the end of each show, my colleagues and I stumbled down the risers, hell-bent on getting to the next show venue in the nick of time which, in real time, would be an hour too early.

Inevitably, a few rogue designers spurned the sterility of the Bryant Park tents and lured the fashion pack to grand architectural gems, like Grand Central Terminal, or to places imbued with history and character like the Apollo Theater, to the swanky Pool Room at the Four Seasons or the Starlight Room at the Waldorf. And there were always one or two misogynist designers who invited us to a Depression-era ballroom or to a dank cobblestone plat below a bridge abutment, on the theory that baleful surroundings will serve as an edgy counterpoint to their sumptuous clothes. One year, Calvin Klein booked a brooding warehouse in the Meat Packing District for a nighttime showing of his spring collection.

The show was scheduled to begin at nine. It wouldn't. It wouldn't start until eleven. Nevertheless, at nine sharp hundreds of us huddled in clots on a gloomy side street where once the blood of lambs stained the gutters. Eventually, security men began trickling guests indoors. I filed into the lobby and followed a group into the freight elevator, an open-walled conveyance overhung with looping chains and pulleys. Somebody yanked a lever. During a lurchy, eight-story ascent we gazed out upon layers of cavernous, bare-wall spaces. Moonlight sluiced through broken window panes. Dust motes swirled in the stale air. The place reeked of death and despair.

At the top, I grabbed a plastic glass of Moet & Chandon and found my seat. The drink was tepid. The rental chair wobbled. The music was loud and awful.

"Look," said a reporter from New Jersey, pointing.

I turned and saw blue-gold flashes of current. Worse, water was dripping from exposed pipes onto the arcing junction box.

"These guys plugged state-of-the-art electronics into Edison-era sockets," my friend said. "For this somebody issued an occupancy permit?"

The show was blessedly brief. Afterward, I elected to forgo the thrills of the freight elevator and joined a crowd twining down eight flights of metal stairs. It was after midnight, chilly, and drizzling. I watched the ladies from *Vogue* and the *New York Times* slide into waiting hire cars and glide off, taking the corner steady as ocean liners. Then a friend and I struck out on foot through the gloaming, laying down our shadows in cones of downlight.

Back at the Paramount Hotel, a little Ian Schrager jewel just off Times Square, a delight delited. Ralph had sent over an invitation to a garden party. A gathering at six the next night at the Cooper-Hewitt Museum, formerly the Andrew Carnegie mansion. A Ralph and Ricky Lauren garden party, at sunset, at an Upper East Side mansion. There was a God in the heavens.

The following evening was gloriously autumn, the air soft, and the breeze benevolent. Taxis formed a queue in front of the mansion and inched forward with uncommon patience. I strolled in with a newspaper friend from California. Our footfalls clicked on the marble floor and echoed to the high ceiling. The central corridor was lined with sharp young men wearing tuxedoes and discreet earphones. "Cheetahs," my friend said, and I nodded. We hurried straight through and down a sweeping staircase to the walled garden.

Waiters bent with trays of fluted champagne, foie gras stuffed figs, and fist-sized strawberries. Arias wafted on night air redolent with the scent of chrysanthemums and late roses. We mingled, coalesced and dispersed again, chatting in the banal way one does, savoring the glamour.

As a reporter, I was trained to add texture and context to my stories, but that night I didn't. I didn't give a moment's thought to the men who had labored most of the day in that garden, erecting a diaphanous tent that rippled now on the slightest breeze. Or the electricians who had wired chandeliers dripping with teardrop crystals so pinpoints of light glowed through the filmy fabric. I didn't think about—and wouldn't be writing about—the carpenters who had assembled the runway, the haulers who had lugged in upholstered banquettes, the caterers who had cored figs and arranged strawberries so they perched equidistant on trays, the dressers drizzling gowns over marble-skinned models, the stylists fiddling needlessly with perfect hair and makeup, whisking away a brooch, adding a feathered barrette. I didn't dwell on them and I wasn't meant to; every trace of effort had been swept away before dusk bathed the garden in apricot light.

The music swelled and then hushed. Ralph beckoned to his guests. Ricky moved to his side. The forty or so guests ambled to the tent and lounged on low banquettes. "Like the ancient Romans," I whispered to a friend.

"Not all of them," she replied.

Then out came a parade of evanescent creatures, lanky blue-eyed blondes staring into the middle distance, prancing like Lipizzaners, gliding like swans in $10,000 gowns that were understated and over the top.

It was soon over, this invitation–only party that was only part party but all show. Out front, guests were alighting from taxis again, a second shift. Caterers were pinching a second batch of figs onto doily–lined trays. Somewhere, stylists were fussing over models stripped to their thong underwear, smoking cigarettes and leafing through *Pravda*. The cheetahs were back, wordlessly inviting us to hit the road.

My friends and I walked through the back gate, as instructed, and lingered on the sidewalk under a tall tree. I noticed a bird on one of the limbs that overhung the garden. As I watched, the bird pivoted its head, as if auditing our return to reality. Odd, I thought, a parrot, here, on 91st Street. It was green, an iridescent lime green with a butter yellow crown and scarlet–tipped wings. I smiled, thinking the magnificent bird was meant to be a sort of farewell to a magical evening.

"See that?" I said.

"The parrot? Yeah, Ralph probably found it on some tropical island and had it brought back."

"For tonight?"

My friend shrugged. "It's possible."

"Bet on it," a passer–by chimed in.

We were still bird-watching, languishing in party's afterglow, when a woman shuffled toward us. She was stooped, her features obscured under a halo of wild hair. Even from a distance we smelled her, a musky damp-basement odor with undertones of piss. A plastic netting sack hung from the crook of her elbow and she kept it close, as if it held items of great import, though we could see it did not.

We stepped off the sidewalk to give way but she paused in our midst. One of my friends scribbled a message in his reporter's notebook and handed it to me. "For every twenty drop-dead gorgeous models at a Ralph Lauren stuffed fig fluted champagne garden party," he wrote, "there's a bag lady."

We moved along. We had deadlines. A dozen fashion shows the next day, a dozen the day after that.

Behind us, the woman whistled a sharp two-note summons. I turned in time to see the bird fly awkwardly to her shoulder. One wing hung at an odd angle, I noticed. Its feathers were patchy, and its eyes were ringed with crust.

At the corner, I flagged a taxi. As it melded into the current of evening traffic, I glanced back. The woman and her bird had crossed Fifth and were continuing on, into Central Park, into the embrace of indifferent night.

The Birdman's Release
Maureen Tolman Flannery

One hot, tropical afternoon
the birdman walks to the shed
where his wares are singing jungle music

in hand-made bamboo cages
built to stack, one upon another,
from floor to cielo.

With palsied fingers
he fumbles to unlatch each diminutive door
and stands erect as his bent spine allows

while tiny gems of quetzal-blue,
emerald, and ruby hover above him,
twittering instructions for flight.

All birds, once released,
perch on his shoulders and arms,
sink needle-talons into the loose weave

of his shabby muslin shirt,
and flap fluorescent rainbows
of synchronized wings

lifting him above the lean-to
where they once confined each other.
Wind plays the Andean flutes

of his airy bones,
and his slack skin flaps
like prayer flags in a gentle breeze.

Young men working in nearby fields
glance up to see him
coloring the clouds with his ascent.

Secret Sadness of Waning Fertility
Maureen Tolman Flannery

These are heartfelt couplings,
the last few chances for our mingling flesh
to draw some uncalculated factor
into an already complex equation.
My dwindling power to call forth independent life
is balance to those early years
when I, a new wife, fecund as a rumor,
bore you more than we had bargained for.

And we know each other's bodies as our own
their only surprise the periodic rise of new keratoses,
brown and scaly as though we would
slowly kiss each other back into toads.
Each time now I assure you I could not conceive.
Then again I flow through one more moon tide,
my body clinging to fertility like a weather-beaten farmer
reluctant to give over his fields.
A tender and blessed love thrives in the darkness
while our unconscious collaboration with the gods
is waning like a harvest moon.

But as we thrust toward fearless years of reckless sex,
there courses in us both,
in lieu of lush fluids of fertility, a secret sadness.
No more amber-haired babies will hover like sea birds,
poised to descend and trouble the waters we enter.
The last of our lovely ones has been remembered unto life.
No more formless unborns tread starlight
beyond the hard matter of our love,
hoping to catch us off guard.

Thunder

Heather Frankland

I will tame the rain one day I will
teach it tricks how to
stand on my shoulder or inner lip.
It will be a tendril curling
across my palm or a dot
of sweat sifting through my hair.
It will be my party trick
when the stars think they're going to shine
when the moon things it'll be praised
I'll draw the rain out. I'll have a code word
for a little rain, average rain, and a Midwestern storm.
The weather guys will be confused
how those orange areas splatter
so easily on their screen.
I will not warn.
I will not tell those I love.
I will not.
The storm will come and wash out
all the oils on the highway—
a skeleton concrete clean drifting.
You'll see after the rain is tamed.
I'll drench you awake.

Incubator
Pat Gallant

Pushed aside into a corner,
the old incubator sits
having given birth through
blood, sweat and tears.

How many babies she carried,
holding them, keeping them warm
and snug, and safe,
breathing in unison
with her small charges.

For years and years
the incubator worked
till she was worn out,
shoved aside
for a newer model—
all but forgotten.
Old, yet she still is...

Though her cords have been cut
and cut again,
If one takes the time to listen,
one can hear her still breathing,
heartbeat by heartbeat,
step-by-step,
trying to keep the rhythm
of her off-spring
long gone.

Nothing Was the Same

Gail Goepfert

Nothing was the same
now that it was fall too soon.

Summer passed
without breezes sifting through
the open window
misting the air with the perfume
of mown grass and flushed children
catching fireflies at dusk.

Nothing was the same
without muggy nights
of summers gone
when standing on the lawn
I waved the garden hose,
an orchestra conductor with her baton,
as the flowers crooned
at the man in the moon.
I longed to soak
in the sweet smell of sultry heat
to welcome
the pulse of the cricket's song
lulling the heavens
into tranquility.

Nothing was the same
when the early chill of fall
stole the music
of summer nights.

Muse on a Gray Day

Gail Goepfert

Pluck a gardenia to plant behind one ear.
Catch a glimpse of a cedar waxwing's
feast in the crabapple's arms.
Weave a basket from coconut fronds.

Sing campfire songs as flames illumine the stars.
Sand down a peach pit to make a ring.
Study the fishing bobber attached
to the line on grandpa's bamboo pole.

Crank the rusted handle on the
homemade ice cream freezer.
Lattice the top and crimp the edges of
the rhubarb pie.
Ignore the mess of making cutout cookies.

Dry off in the afterglow of swimming a mile.
Uncurl the fingers from the handlebars at the end
of an all-day ride.
Pamper the feet that hiked 17 miles for
a Mississippi catfish dinner.

Kiss the apple of the baby's cheek and
inhale the scent of her skin.
Stroke the matted teddy in the rocking chair.
Reread letters penned by well-remembered
hands

On a gray day lest we forget.

Strip Tease
Peter Goodwin

Snow falls, covering the land
thaws, freezes, and more snow falls
thaws, freezes, and snows some more
layers of snow
obscuring   flattening   covering
the land two feet and more
the weight of winter
pressing on the land.

It snows and thaws and thaws some more
and as it thaws , hidden layers emerge
revealing a past history
an archeology in white and shadow:
gentle animals tracks crisscrossing
ski tracks so straight
recalling days bright and clear
foot steps. large ungainly holes
recalling unwilling errands
through heavy unforgiving winter

the footsteps slowly expanding
leading to bare ground
bare ground hinting at a Spring to come
the land slowly shedding its winter coats
a slow motion strip tease
revealing fresh green grass
and beckoning daffodils
ready to burst open.

Gram's Story
Mary Ann Grzych

Grandma greeted me at the door with a big, comforting hug. She was much taller than my five foot four, and her long, strong arms completely encircled me. "I'm so glad to see you, Julie," she said. "Come out to the kitchen. I'm in the middle of baking an apple pie."

Gram's apple pies were legendary. My mouth watered at the thought of it. "I'd love to watch you; maybe I can discover your secret. No matter how hard I try, I just can't get the crust as tender as yours."

She led me by the hand toward her sunny yellow-and-white kitchen. I loved that room. It was the scene of many special childhood memories. Family dinners in the dining room were elegant, but suppers in Gram's kitchen were my favorite. Before supper we often gathered around her antique oak table, talking and savoring the smell of whatever was baking in the oven. No matter what it was, we knew it would be good.

"You're just in time to peel the apples," she said, as she handed me a paring knife and took out the chilled pie dough from the frig. "I've already made the dough for this pie, but if we have time, we can make another for you to take home."

"It's a deal," I said, grabbing a big, juicy Macintosh and one of the old, blue-striped, crockery bowls Gram always used. "I saw a set of these bowls at an antique shop last week. They're collectors' items now."

"Everything in this old house is becoming a collector's item including me, Julie," she replied with a deep, throaty laugh. She took her glass rolling pin from its nesting place.

"That's one thing I've never seen in any antique shop, Gram," I said, pointing to the rolling pin.

"It belonged to your grandfather's mom," she replied, running her hand lovingly along the cloudy glass. "She taught me to make pies in this very same kitchen." She paused; a strange, hesitant look crossed her face. She looked first at me then back at the rolling pin not saying a word. The silence and the pained expression on her face unnerved me.

"What's wrong, Gram?" I asked softly.

"I need to tell you something—something that I've put off for too long." She took a deep breath, squared her broad shoulders and said, "You know how much I love you, Julie. You're the most important person in the world to me, and now I have to tell you that I'm not exactly the person you think I am."

My heart started pounding and the knife fell from my hand, as I saw the serious look on her face. "Don't tell me that you're not my Gram!" I exclaimed. I slipped off the stool, retrieved the knife and quickly headed for the sink. I had a bad feeling about this conversation. What did that mean—she's not the person I think she is? Gram waited until I washed the knife and returned to my seat across the counter from her before continuing.

"No, I'm not going to tell you that I'm not your Gram," she assured me. "You do need to hear my story though, while I'm still able to tell it.

"I was born in Hartford, Connecticut, January 29, 1935 to Joseph and Anna Frey, their first child after five years of marriage. I was a belated gift and much heralded by many aunts, uncles, and cousins."

"Frey?" I interrupted, puzzled. That was a name I didn't recognize.

"Yes, Frey," she said. "You'll see. My christening was a huge celebration. Everyone in the family showed up at the church to welcome James into the family."

I let out a gasp, but before I could say anything she rushed on.

"Yes, James. Not Jean. I spent the first 22 years of my life living a spiritual lie. Biologically I was a boy, then a man, but from the time I was a little kid I knew deep down inside that was wrong. I went to bed every night praying that in the morning I'd wake up, look in the bathroom mirror and see a beautiful girl looking back at me."

Gram's eyes began to tear at the memory. I was stunned into silence. I didn't know what to say or do, so I started to peel the apple in my hand. I needed a moment to absorb some of this so she wouldn't see how shocked I was. I wanted to dash outside, walk up her sidewalk, ring the bell and start the day all over again, but I realized Gram needed my support. I put down the apple, rested my elbows on the counter, leaned toward her, my hands cupping my chin and gave her my full attention.

"I was miserable," she continued. "When I was little, I got cars and trucks for Christmas, but I secretly coveted the beautiful dolls my little sister, Marge, got. When I was a teenager, everyone expected me to date this girl, or that friend's daughter. I wanted none of it. My stomach churned every time the subject came up. I wanted to scream at them, 'Can't you see I'm really a girl?' But, of course, I didn't. I couldn't. I swallowed my unhappiness for years, even thought about ending the misery several times, but didn't have the courage."

She gave a little sob, then put the pie dough back in the refrigerator, wiped her hands on her apron, poured two cups of coffee and sat on the stool across from me.

I sipped the hot coffee, not tasting it. My head spun with questions. How could she be my Gram, if she was born a man? She couldn't have given birth to my mom. I resisted the urge to blurt out my questions and reached across to take her free hand in mine. I hoped she didn't see me staring at her Adam's apple. I hadn't noticed before how pronounced it was for a woman. I gave her hand a little squeeze. She smiled feebly and stared down at her wrinkled, age-spotted hands.

"I was at a loss for what to do—completely clueless," Gram said. "Then in 1952, a woman named Christine Jorgenson hit the headlines in Europe and here in the U.S. She, too, had been born a male, and after years of therapy, hormone treatments, and several operations, she physically became what she'd always known was true. She was a woman. Her story gave me the courage to go to Denmark and plead with her doctors to do the same for me."

I gasped again, but she didn't seem to notice. She went on. "My parents, your great-grandparents, were devastated when I told them what I intended to do. My brother, who I'd always trusted to stand up for me, refused to hear any of it. 'He's nuts,' he said. 'We should have him declared and committed.' I found out years later that's what some families in those days actually did to children like me."

Gram paused for moment, the pain pinching her face. "I think my family considered it, though in the end they settled for an oath of secrecy. 'What will people think? We'll be ashamed to show our faces around town,' was all I heard, and I was long past caring what people thought, and willing to go it on my own. I packed a small bag and left the next day before dawn without telling anyone." She paused, her body tensed and I heard Gram's neck crack as she closed her eyes and turned her head from side to side before continuing.

"I got a job in New York City, saved every penny I could until I had enough to go to Denmark. My knees actually buckled as I boarded the plane that I hoped would take me to myself—my real self. I won't go into the details, but the trip was all that I had hoped. I spent over two years in Denmark. On my return flight, I wore a dress, nylons, and two inch heels. My shoulder length, blonde hair bounced with every step. I felt great and loved the smiles from the men on the plane as I sauntered to my seat. The man across the aisle offered to put my carry-on in the overhead bin and I let him."

Gram paused again, refilled our cups. She looked straight into my eyes, as if trying to read my reaction. "Go on Gram," I said. My questions could wait.

"I'd had no contact with my family since the day I left Hartford. I sent them a letter after I arrived in New York telling them that I was happy, healthy, and biologically and legally Jean Frey. I enclosed my address, but never heard from them. I got a job at an ad agency in Manhattan, and that's where I met your grandfather. I think we were attracted to each other right away. At first we just exchanged small talk, and then had coffee together. Joe told me he had been divorced for two years and had a daughter—your mother. We went to dinner and the theater on our first date. He brought me yellow roses," she said pointing to a vase of fresh ones on the kitchen table.

"I'll tell you more later, if you want me to, but the short version is we fell in love. I had to tell him about my surgery. I agonized over it for days, afraid that I'd lose him, like I'd lost my family. But he listened quietly then took me in his arms and said, 'I love you. The rest doesn't matter.'

"After we were married, we settled in Fairfield, Connecticut to be near his widowed mother who lived here in Southport. When she became ill, we moved into this house to take care of her. Southport still had small town, Puritan values, so the details of my former life were never discussed. We never even told your mom and dad."

She pursed her lips slightly, then as if she was reading my mind she said, "You're wondering why I'm telling you this now. Why not continue to keep the secret? I might have, but two days ago a private detective, a Mr. Filmore, rang my doorbell. He asked if I was Jean Frey. It took me by surprise. I hadn't heard that name in years. He said my family in Hartford had hired him to find me. My mind flashed back to that night before I walked out, and their hateful threats tore me apart all over again. Why would they pay someone to find me after all these years?

"Once we were seated in the living room, Mr. Filmore handed me a small, white envelope from my mother. I sat there for a moment staring at it.

"My heart pounded as I lifted out this single page letter," Gram said, as she passed it over to me. I read:

Dear Jean,

Your sister, Margaret, has stage-four leukemia and needs a bone marrow transplant. Everyone in the family has been tested and Margaret is on the national transplant list, but time is running out. I know that I don't have the right to ask anything of you. But I am. I'm hoping that you'll agree to be tested as a possible donor. Please don't hold my failure to support you against Margaret. She was just a child when you left and knows nothing of the reasons for your leaving.

I've never forgotten you, but it has taken me years to think of you as Jean. I've tried to understand what you must have been going through and hope the years have softened my soul. Mr. Filmore has all the details about what is involved in being a bone marrow donor. I pray you'll give this gift to your sister. Whatever you decide, I still pray for you and love you, Jean.

"Oh, my gosh. What did you do, Gram?"

Her body tensed and she spat the words out with a vehemence I had never heard in her voice before.

"I sat there stunned for what seemed an eternity. I was dumbfounded. The hypocrisy of that woman overwhelmed me. I didn't buy a word of my mother's apology. Love me? Love me?" He face twisted with an ugliness I'd never seen there before. "She didn't even sign the letter, Mom! All those painful years I lived as a boy—the way my family wanted no part of me when I told them— it all hit me again."

She reached into the apple bowl and sat rubbing her hand back and forth over one before continuing the story.

"Finally, Mr. Filmore broke the silence," she said. "He took a big manila envelope from his briefcase, and told me that all the pertinent information about bone marrow transplants was there. As he left, he told me to call him if I had any further questions.

"I kept busy cooking, cleaning—anything to keep from opening the envelope. By evening, I couldn't put it off any longer. I settled into my easy chair and opened the envelope.

"I read the information over and over throughout the night trying to digest it all. What I read frightened me for Margie. The last time I'd seen her she was a healthy, curly haired kid roller skating or playing ball in the park; usually with a band-aid on one knee or the other. It's hard to imagine her with a life threatening illness, but the truth is that she'll die without the transplant. By morning I knew that I had to call you, Julie. And tell you my story."

She leaned back on the stool; with her shoulders lowering, I saw some of the tension drain from her body. She seemed tired, but relieved.

I looked out the kitchen window at Gram's garden; at the yellow roses on the table. I couldn't begin to wrap my mind around what she had told me about herself. That would take time.

"Will you be tested, Gram?"

"I was, yesterday. I'm a match."

"What are you going to do?" I asked, taking her hand in mine again.

She sighed, looked off into space and replied softly, "The only thing I can."

winter mirror/cheval glass

juley harvey

gray days at the beach
seem like a flying bonus,
a waddling gift, something saying
it's always sunny,
so we'll give you this,
a change of pace, peace, for your money,
guess what we're gonna do next.
and is the light more beautiful
straight gold, or filtered through
pearly clouds that glow,
the color of dolphins
and whales, sleek and wet,
and sea-maid memories,
old fishermen's tales,
oceans above,
sky below?
the less color,
the more promise,
spotlights of silver
beamed onto
gleaming, green-eyed waves,
baring their bathed hope chests
of bones and dreams.

Water, Wind and Sun
Nancy J. Heggem

Water
We build our villages and towns beside the water,
port for ships in trade, or fishing fleets,
safe harbor for the lost, the poor, the immigrant.
Running water turned the mill wheel, ground our grain.
Rushing water helped turn our forests into lumber.
Big water, falling water we call on your
power to light our cities, run our machines.

Wind
Honored, respected from earth's four corners,
put to work by Holland's crafty low-landers.
Windmills carefully packed and brought across the ocean.
Wooden towers marked civilization as we crossed the prairie;
arms turning, pumping water hidden deep in the earth.
The new crop, rising like giant steel daffodils, turn their face west.
These turbines on coast and valley bring power.

Sun
Ancestors honored you as God.
Built their hogans and faced you each morning.
Laid their bricks in your golden light to cure.
Our fields of grain and trees of fruit
turn you energy into food for the people.
Now we have built cells eight feet by eight
to capture your energy, heat our water, light our homes.

Chicago, Chicago, New York, New York
Julie A. Jacob

For eight years in the 1990s, I lived in a high rise apartment building on Lake Shore Drive in Chicago called the New York. Perhaps the developers thought it gave the building a certain cachet to name it for a place on a map, like the Dakota in the real New York, or maybe they thought the name would give the building a dash of Manhattan mystique. Whatever the reason, it worked. Almost everyone I met in Chicago during those years had heard of the New York, had read about it, asked what it was like to live there.

The New York was one of those ostentatious high-rises built in the 1980s, a skinny building, 44 stories tall, tan and brown brick, wider in the back than the front, like the V formation of migrating geese, so that nearly all the apartments had a spectacular view of Lake Michigan. That was one of the big draws of the place; you could see the lake from almost every one of the 500 apartments. Two lighted stone porticos about 10 feet high flanked the long driveway that swept up to the two-story glass-canopied entrance. They looked like lighthouses or massive penises, take your pick.

A stream of cabs stopped at the entrance all hours of the day and night dropping off and picking up residents and guests. Inside the doorway, uniformed doormen ensconced behind a massive marble desk guarded the entrance with the zealousness of Rottweilers. They were no minimum-wage grunts dozing by a radio; the apartment manager told me that most of the doormen were off-duty police officers, and no one got into the building without their approval.

The lobby was an ode to the opulence of the Decade of Greed. It had a soaring, sky-lit ceiling and a marble floor that was notoriously slippery in the winter. Just inside the doorway, a row of stainless steel balls hung suspended from steel cables; they clicked and bobbed like metronomes in a curving cement trough through which a thin ribbon of water trickled. A polished piano gleamed in front of a huge tan and black abstract painting that covered the west wall. Mornings and evenings, Mondays through Fridays, a pale, elegant man with thinning blond hair, clad in a tuxedo, played light pleasant music to soothe the residents as they trudged back through the lobby in the evenings with exhausted eyes and heavy briefcases. The pianist seemed wistful as he played; I wondered if he felt sad that his years of training had culminated in being a human Muzak machine to the yuppies who passed him each evening without a glance.

Often people I met at cocktail parties or volleyball asked me where I lived. "Oh, Lake Shore and Waveland," I'd say.

"The New York?" the acquaintance would ask, eyebrows raised, "What's it like inside? Is it really nice? Wow, it must be cool to live there."

"Yes," I'd nod, feeling like a fraud, because of the implication that you had to have money to live there when, in fact, the rents for studios and one-bedroom apartments were surprisingly affordable, at least for the small units without balconies on the lower floors, like mine. It was 1992 and vacant units in upscale apartment buildings glutted the market, so I got a good deal on the rent.

My apartment, number 704, was a trim 600 square feet, long and narrow like a boxcar with a postage stamp-sized kitchen, but it had huge closets and a fantastic view. It faced north and east, and when I stood at the bay window in the living room in the morning, coffee mug in hand, I could see the cars zipping by on Lake Shore Drive, the softball diamonds in Waveland Park, and the old brick clubhouse with the clock tower near the first hole of Waveland Golf Course. Beyond it, Lake Michigan unfurled in shimmering waves of blue or green or gray, depending on the season and time of day. The lake was always beautiful, summer or winter, cloudy or sunny. I never tired of looking at it.

From the other window, the narrow one facing west, I could see the house, apartments, and churches stretching west on Waveland Avenue and watch the splashes of red and orange light spill across the rooftops at sunset. Wrigley Field was three blocks west of the New York; I couldn't see it from my floor, but at night, with my windows open, I could hear the crowds cheer. The sound lulled me to sleep many nights, like waves or crickets chirping.

My apartment never felt like home. It was too small and too neutral to ever feel like anything other than a glorified hotel room. No matter how many pictures I hung on the wall and how artfully I arranged my furniture, I couldn't disguise the industrial gray carpeting and stark white walls. Outside my door, the hallways reminded me of a hotel, too: freshly vacuumed, tastefully decorated in shades of deep blue and cream and utterly anonymous. In the eight years that I lived there, I rarely saw another person in the hallway. When my friend Katie visited from Wisconsin, she insisted that she didn't believe anyone else really lived on my floor because she never saw or heard anyone else. I eventually met two people on my floor—a woman who lived next door for a few years and an older woman who lived at the end of the hall and gave voice lessons for a living.

Those two, along with an elderly man whom I'd see on the elevator with his overweight bulldog, were the only ones who ever smiled or said hello to me. Everyone else I knew only as a muffled door shutting far down the hallway, the back of a trench coat disappearing into a doorway, or an expressionless person in the elevator.

I didn't really mind the lack of conviviality inside, at least not at first, at least not at that time of my life, because the New York was not a place where you lived if you wanted to stay inside. It was a place you lived to experience life outside its doors. The New York was marketed as a place for active urban professionals. The newspaper ads showed pictures of handsome, youthful people playing tennis, jogging, or sipping coffee at an outdoor cafe.

I must have fit the targeted demographic, because what I remember most vividly about my life at the New York is constantly moving, coming and going, on my way to this or that. I would hurry through the lobby in the evening, shoe heels clicking on the marble floor, and say to Duke, the burly ex-cop and doorman, "Hi, Duke, could you please turn on the cab light? Thank you." I would stand outside the lobby in the dry, cold air of a winter's night, in jeans and a turtleneck sweater, hands pressed in the pockets of my leather jacket, stamping my boots on the cement, waiting for the cab to pull in the driveway. I'd get in and say, "The corner of Clark and Diversey, please" if I was going to dinner with my crowd of friends at the Italian restaurant we liked, or "Seminary and Wrightwood" if I was visiting my friends Allen and Billy, or "Southport and Greenleaf" if I was headed to my writing workshop.

Sometimes I had to give directions to the cabdriver on the way to someplace, but I never, ever had to give directions on the way home. "Thirty-six sixty North Lake Shore Drive" was all I had to say and the cab driver immediately knew where to go.

"The New York, right?" the cab driver would ask.

"Yes, the New York."

"Nice building," the driver would say as he sped north on Lake Shore Drive. The cab drivers always drove me north to my apartment, never south, because due to my Lakeview neighborhood snobbishness, the city north of Irving Park Road simply did not exist for me. Irving Park was the dividing line where the civilized streets of Lakeview ended and the wilderness of Uptown began. No one I knew who lived in Lakeview or Lincoln Park ever ventured further north than Irving Park Road at that time. Uptown and Edgewater was where you lived if you couldn't afford to live in Lakeview, or if you were an adventurous urban pioneer leading the wave of gentrification.

On sticky summer evenings I loped through the lobby wearing sweat shorts and a faded t-shirt from my coed volleyball league, headed out for a bike ride or walk along the lake.

On gray January afternoons I brushed the snow off my coat before entering the lobby, back from seeing a movie at Landmark Century Cinema—usually something artsy or foreign—with a friend or playing a game of volleyball at the Lincoln Park High School gym.

After awkward dates, I would bolt out on my date's car and dash into the lobby, pausing only to say a quick hello to Duke. Other nights, heart pounding with excitement, I would wait impatiently for a cab in the lobby to take me to a date with a man I really liked.

Sometimes my friends and I would go to the black-tie fundraisers sponsored by Lincoln Park Young Professionals or one of the other groups popular with young Chicagoans. Afterwards, I would walk through the lobby at 2 a.m., silent and empty except for the whir of the floor polishing machine operated by the impassive-faced night janitor. My feet would ache, my panty hose would be snagged, and I'd smell of smoke. Sometimes I'd be smiling, after a night that was fun, feeling lucky to be part of this pulsing, interesting urban life. Other times I'd be frowning, trying to convince myself that the $125 ticket had been worth it for two glasses of wine and two hours of trying to make conversation with strangers.

I hurried through that lobby every day: to work, volleyball games, exercise classes, writing workshops, movies, plays, happy hours, parties, dinners, and dates. Sometimes, looking back now, I am not sure now what I was trying to accomplish. Perhaps I was trying to make up for the fun times I'd missed in my twenties, when I had been broke and slogging my way through graduate school. I thought it was pointless to live in a big city if you weren't going to take advantage of all that it offered.

I lived in that apartment for eight years. I never thought I would stay so long in a building that felt like a hotel, but it was so easy, so convenient, to live there. The Number 146 express bus to downtown stopped in front of the building. The grocery store was around the corner. The lakefront bike path was across the street. And so I stayed and stayed, and my life moved on through most of my thirties in a whirl of the activities enjoyed by single people in Chicago with a little money in their pockets, and my apartment served as my base to sleep and eat. Every September I'd find my lease renewal notice under my door, every year I took a desultory glance at condos for sales, and every year I re-signed my lease.

Then one year I found a notice under my door stating that the New York was converting to a condominium. The price for my bland box was $169,000, as is. It wasn't worth the price.

It was time to say good-bye to my life in the New York.

My cheerful realtor began showing me one condo after another which I rejected one by one. Too dark, no view, ugly bathroom, tiny, lacked security, terrible location. I marvel at my realtor's patience at my pickiness.

When I had given up ever finding a place that I would really like and was resigned to renting someplace else, I found my home. I walked into a one-bedroom condo in an art deco building on Marine Drive, three miles north of the New York, smack in the middle of Uptown, and fell in love. The condo could not have been more different than the New York. The plumbing was old, the closets were small, and the elevator was slow. The neighborhood was miles away from the bustle of Lakeview, but the building had a charming, flower-filled courtyard with a glass brick art deco fountain and frosted glass art deco sconces and tiled mosaic walls in the lobby. My unit had just been rehabbed top to bottom, and my new home was light and airy with gleaming oak parquet floors, 10-foot ceilings, fresh ivory paint, track lights, granite windowsills and birch cabinets. It was as sweet and inviting as a dollhouse. It was across the street from the park and bike path, and I could even see a sliver of the lake from the bedroom window. Most of all, it was all mine.

So in December 2000, I stood one last time in my apartment, now stripped down to its white walls and gray carpeting, and stood at the bay window and gazed one last time at that beautiful view of Lake Michigan. Then I walked out and began my life in my new home.

My life changed after I moved to Marine Drive. I quickly got to know my neighbors. Unlike the New York, this building was filled with a delightful potpourri of residents: an architect and his wife, a flautist, who lived with their baby daughter on the floor above me, an elderly African-American woman with a merry shih tzu; a Hispanic gay man on the first floor who listened to pulsating Latin techno-pop music, a pet photographer with a sweet little pug named Pig; an interracial lesbian couple, an Hawaiian woman who made quilts, and a family from Thailand. People smiled. They said hello and chatted. I had moved from an anonymous, homogenous hotel to an eclectic, quirky village, and I loved it.

I still met my friends for dinner and movies and drinks, I still stood in the lobby waiting for a cab. I still rode my bike along the lake and took long walks by the beach. But I no longer felt that desire to be out and about, doing and moving, all the time. I was content to spend an afternoon at home, painting the walls or hanging pictures or learning to cook. My life felt less exciting, but more solid.

Two framed pictures of the view of Waveland Park and Lake Michigan, as seen from the bay window in my apartment at the New York—one taken in the winter, the other in the summer—now sit on a shelf in my condo. I have them to remind me, not only of the view, but of that place where I lived for eight years, when I was young and new to the city and all the promise and excitement of Chicago lay outside my door.

Hard

Allan Johnston

A hard gray, the lake has entangled the skies—
gulls, winds, waves, clouds—
this face of wrath too windy to read,
the rain not yet born.

This is how it is in moments
when it becomes clear what you will not do.
Death wears a similar face to weather—
obstructive, constant, fickle.
A wind turned on and off.

The sun continues beyond these clouds
unconnected to hope
except in the way a rolling coin
joins to effects of sidewalks—
cracks and imperfections denying
distance.

                              Things simplify—
eating, breathing, taking a walk,
tying a shoe—

the weather widens

the waves hit the shore,
angry pillows of water
slapped on a bed

in the dazed moments before some sleep.

Dragons, Sledgehammers, Sequins and High Heels
Gary Jugert

Elaine carried the laptop into the kitchen and heaved it onto the table smiling as if she'd just bought Lady Gaga tickets.

"Hey. Dad left his computer on and look what he's been working on." She rotated the computer. Everyone, except Granny, could see a three-dimensional gaming environment "He's been playing Seasons of Change and look at his avatar. He's a girl."

"Elaine, go put that back. Stay out of my office." Robert's face reddened a bit. He glared at his daughter, but her stringy black hair obscured her eyes from view.

"You're a girl?" Jimmy asked and leaned his skinny body across the kitchen table to peer into the computer screen.

"Elaine, go put that away!" The edge in Robert's voice sounded angry.

"Why are you a girl? Shouldn't you be a boy?" Elaine ignored her father's command.

"Elaine, honey, go put the computer back and stay out of your father's office. Wash your hands, dinner is ready." Maggie placed a large bowl of mashed potatoes in front of Granny. "Here you go, Mom," she yelled. "Be careful; it's hot." She glanced up at her husband over her half-frame reading glasses. "And do tell Robert, why on Earth are you pretending to be a girl?"

"Elaine! Put the computer back." Then, as if trying to change the subject, he said, "Mashed potatoes again? Really?"

"Look, Dad even gave her a belly button ring and tattoos." Jimmy's Led Zeppelin T-shirt hung down into the green beans as he crawled onto the table trying to see.

"She's so detailed, Dad; like a Barbie doll only way better. You made her look hot." Elaine continued to ignore her parents. "Is this what you wished Mom looked like?"

"Elaine! Now! Put the computer back." Robert pushed his ample girth out of the vinyl kitchen chair steadying himself with his meaty fingers on the edge of the table, but Elaine grabbed the laptop and dashed away giggling.

"Well? Is that how you want me to look?" A smile crept across her tired face. Her hair straggled down around her face escaping from her morning efforts to subdue those natural curls. A day of teaching and an evening of being the chef and housemaid for her family took its toll on Maggie's coiffure. Robert straightened out his flannel shirt, and shook his head. "Do you want a girlfriend that looks like her, Bob?"

Jimmy shoveled out a huge portion of green beans and stared at his father waiting to hear the answer.

"Bobby has a girlfriend?" Granny raised her head away from her meal, wrinkled her brow, and stared down to the far end of the short table to see what she could of her fat son-in-law. Her oversized eye glasses magnified her eyeballs making her look like a bug. Her dated hearing aids and missing front teeth accentuated the impression.

"No, Mother," Maggie yelled. "He's pretending to be a girl."

Granny's attention returned to the plate in front of her. "Oh. Even when you married him, I thought he was a twink."

"He's not gay, Mom, he's ... oh never mind." Maggie's voice trailed off. She finished helping her mother cut her food, sat down, and looked across the table at her son. "Eat your beans, Jimmy. Robert, did you even think about making your avatar look like me?"

Elaine returned to the kitchen. "Boy Dad, I checked out other players in that game and you spent way more time than anybody else on your girl. Perfect shoes, perfect clothes, and my gosh— that hair. You must have spent hours. You built the ultimate example of sexy."

"Sit down and eat your dinner." Maggie pushed the brisket toward her daughter. "So did you, Robert? Try to make an avatar that looked like your wife? Or did you just go for the bimbo straight away?"

Robert opened his mouth to speak, but Granny mumbled under her breath, "In my day all the twinks lived in New York."

"Granny thinks you're gay, Dad." Elaine beamed at her father.

"Or San Francisco," Granny continued.

"When did you turn gay?" Maggie's lips twisted into an ironic smile. Robert tossed his napkin onto the table and pushed away from the table. "Oh, come off it, Bob; we're just teasing you."

"I'm going to the pub. Jimmy, you deal with these three." Robert lumbered from the house into the garage. He tucked himself into his compact auto and his awkward hands twisted the ignition key, but it groaned and made a clicking noise. He hadn't left the house in weeks and the battery must have died. "Goddammit." He tugged himself up and out of the tiny vehicle and glanced around the mess of cardboard boxes. Jimmy's motor scooter sat on its center stand amid the chaos. He flipped the kill switch to "On," clumsily kicked the starter, the tiny engine buzzed to life, and oily blue smoke filled the garage.

Robert forced his left leg up and over the seat and burdened the little bike with his weight. As he twisted the accelerator Jimmy appeared at the garage door with a look of helpless shock on his face. Robert ignored him and continued on his way.

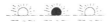

"What'll it be, Bobby?" the bartender asked.

"A pint of stout and silence."

Jubilee pulled the elaborate wooden handle on the beer tap and filled the frozen glass with black syrupy liquid. She tossed down a cardboard square and then set the brew down in front of Robert with a clunk. She leaned against the bar tucking her elbows and hands under her enormous breasts. "Tough day at the office, eh?"

"Tough day at home." Robert stared at Jubilee's cleavage and then up to her eyes. She raised her eyebrows. "Ah, you know, I'm designing modules for a video game called Seasons of Change. Girls have much better powers than boys to encourage female players. I was working on one of my female characters and my daughter showed it to whole family. Now I'm gay." Robert took a long pull on his beer. "Just because you're a girl in a video game doesn't mean you're gay."

Jubilee nodded agreeably.

"It just means you're a girl in a video game. You're not gay. You're not a twink. You're not whatever people think you are. You're just playing a video game with a female character. That's it." Jubilee smiled as Robert's passionate speech rambled from thought to thought: You're not weird. You're not creepy. You're not hiding from real life in your house while your wife supports the family. You're just working on a video game module.

"Sounds like you've thought it through." Jubilee watched Robert's first pint vanish and pulled him a second. "You're playing out a fantasy?"

"Hell, no," Robert raised his voice and his mug at the same time. "Maybe some guys are into that stuff, but not me. It's just a game to me. Don't start sounding like my family."

Jubilee said nothing. The pub became quiet. A faint smell of an exotic perfume wafted across the room. "You seem a little sensitive, old man," a tiny, raspy voice said. Robert glanced behind him to find a troll-like creature with black kinky hair, dark skin, and woolen outerwear. "Why not try out your fantasies in real life?"

Robert turned away from the old woman. "I'll be fine, Cardinia. I think I'll just head on home."

"So soon?" Jubilee asked.

Cardinia sidled up close to Robert. He stared down into his stout, shaking his head. "Listen to a wrinkled old Paki, dear boy." Cardinia's gaze fixed onto Robert like a laser-scoped rifle. "I can help you make things right."

"Nothing is wrong, Cardinia." Robert continued gazing into his pint as if it were a crystal ball.

"Surrounded by women so much stronger than you, and you're fine, eh?" The miniature dark skinned woman with the peculiar odor chuckled to herself. "When I was young and beautiful, I lived in Bombay and worked in the film industry. Stage make-up, beautiful hair-dos, costumes. Movie stars." Cardinia smiled as if seeing herself in a younger body, in a far away land, doing work she loved. "I still know how to make somebody into somebody else."

Robert rolled his neck around and gazed at the old woman as if making a silent agreement. Cardinia pulled a small vial from her satchel and spritzed a miniscule amount of perfume into the air. The odor around Cardinia intensified and the lights from the bar created a glittery effect in the mist. "Let's make their dreams come true."

Robert had never been into the apartments above the pub, but now he stood blurry and naked on a wooden box in one of those upstairs units. He could smell curry.

Cardinia scurried about her flat periodically refilling her glass from a green bottle while unearthing the dusty tools of her craft. She mumbled to herself holding court with the inanimate object around her. "There you are!" ..."Oh my, I'd forgotten about this one!" ..."How did you end up over here!" She'd coaxed him out of his clothing, measured him like a tailor, and began her work on every detail. Hair removal, foundations, fake this and that, scraps of cloth, leather and buckles.

She found an extravagant brunette wig with cascading billowy beauty to flounce about on his shoulders. She plucked his eyebrows into a perfect movie star arch. She rouged his cheeks, purpled his eyelids, and perfumed his neck.

After strapping into a contraption designed to create the illusion of a cleavage, he slid into a silky laced undergarment and a provocative low-cut blouse. His arms looked pretty in lace sleeves with complicated black widow patterns. After many attempts to salvage his ample belly button with baubles and waxes, Cardinia gave up and chose a high-waisted skirt with an oversized, sequined belt. "It's the sequins, my dear, that make the look," she said. Robert objected to the pretty panties, fishnet stockings, and dangerous high heels, but Cardinia insisted. "A woman's outer luxury requires inner beauty."

A kilogram of assorted faux-jewels draped around Robert's body brought the design to completion. Hours after beginning the project, the Paki added the final props: Weapons. Guns and knives and nefarious looking explosives. Then she presented a mirror to Robert. "My god, you've done it. I look just like her."

"The Warrior Princess, courtesy of the drunken Pakistani; you're the most powerful woman in the world." Cardinia's smile suggested she took pleasure in reviving her old skills. "Go home. It's morning."

Robert rode home on the scooter struggling to keep the wig in place with one hand. He parked in the driveway and adjusted the girly accoutrement blown willy-nilly during his ride.

He started up the walkway when the front door flew open and Elaine screamed backward into the house. "See you later. Call me if you find Dad." She hopped down the first step and then stopped dead. "Hi. Can I help you?" she said to the woman standing on her front sidewalk. Robert said nothing. He stared into the suspicious dark eyes of the girl dressed head to toe in black. And then her jaw dropped, her face lit up, and her hand reached up to pull her hair behind her ear. "Oh, my god. Oh, my god." A car pulled up out in the street and honked. "I have to go." Elaine threw her arms around her father, hugged him like she hadn't in many years, and then pulled back. "Gotta go to work. You're gonna freak everyone out." Then she dashed away to catch her ride. "Still love you," she yelled from the window as the car pulled away.

Robert smiled and walked up into the house. Granny sat on the sofa under her hand-crocheted shawl she'd made decades earlier when she still had mastery over her mind, her hands, and her vision. The morning news blared from the television. For the first time in months, Robert sat next to her.

The old woman squinted through her thick lenses. "Who are you?"

"Robert," he said, but not loud enough for her to hear.

"Bobby's girlfriend?" Granny asked. Robert smiled and nodded in an exaggerated "yes" motion.

"Ack. Always thought he was light in the loafers, but if he can get himself a pretty thing like you, he's not what I thought." Granny looked him up and down. "My sister-in-law was fat like you, too—died at 50. You better move fast or get out of here. Bobby's still married to my daughter...for now."

Robert stood and headed into the kitchen, "Maggie!"

"Are you kidding me?" Robert heard yelling from the kitchen. "You stay out all night; don't call. I'm worried sick and you have the nerve to come waltzing in here at...." Maggie saw Robert enter the kitchen and lost her voice.

"Good morning." Robert said, pulling the coffee pot out of its cradle and filling his favorite mug.

"Dad?" Jimmy's eyes widened in terror.

Robert sat down in his usual chair and stared back at his wife and son. "Everyone sleep okay?"

Jimmy pushed away from the table. "I'm going to school." He ran out of the house.

"It's Saturday," Maggie yelled after him. She swiveled around in anger at her husband. "Do you see what you're doing to him?" She ran after her son.

Robert carried the coffee mug into his office, turned on the computer, and logged into Seasons of Change. His young female avatar popped up and gazed vacantly ahead in handcrafted beauty. "Don't we look lovely today?"

Hours later Maggie returned home and sat next to her husband as he stared into the computer game. She was smoking a cigarette. "Jimmy only ran to the end of the block. I took him out for breakfast."

"And started smoking again," Robert said.

"We need to talk about what's happening with you."

Robert fluffed his brunette 'do, one wavy lock falling on his forehead. They both stared into the computer monitor watching a scene of a dozen anachronistic characters conspiring to kill a dragon.

"Are you that girl with the high heels and the sledge hammer?" Maggie asked. As she spoke, Robert pulled his hands away from the keyboard and the diminutive Barbie doll found herself consumed in a fiery inferno emitting from the dragon's nostrils. Her health meter dropped; she fell to the ground. A skull and crossbones appeared on the screen.

"Used to be; not anymore." Robert said with resignation in his voice.

"Why did you let her die?"

"All great characters die at the end of their stories." Robert turned to his wife. Her shoulders slumped and her head drooped in misery. He smiled. "I think I'll be a robot now."

My Dinner with Andrea

Carol Kanter

Running late for a play, my friend
scrapes our still-warm meals
into to-go containers, stacks these

in a bag stamped with restaurant logo
and wonders aloud, Will this food overcook
in the heat the boxes trap?

She nods once, and adds,
Convection is the most useful thing
I learned in high school.

Not in high school physics where laws
made sense and formulas made work,
but in all of high school

while I was busy learning what?
How to seem most likely to succeed,
to read only what's assigned,

how guys make better friends—
habit-forming lessons
I had to unlearn

before the curtain could go up on Life—
unlike the laws of thermodynamics
which if they can be recalled

you can count on
in a timeless sort of way.

62

A Side of Bacon
Amber Kemppainen

Sweat gathered on his brow as he maintained his rhythm: hips pistoning forward. He studied the female under him critically. The faint crow's feet creasing the skin around her eyes puzzled him. He put her age a little under thirty. The odds were still good, though a younger specimen was definitely preferable. With experienced fingers, he teased her nipples through the thin cotton of her shirt. Her breathing quickened, sounding harsh through the fabric of her mask and he pulled her legs up over his shoulders in response. Satisfied, he increased his pace slightly as he felt the muscles quiver in her midsection: it would be soon.

By now it was automatic, this quick perusal of female flesh as they responded to his ministrations. Every hitch of breath, a slight tensing or relaxing of muscle were signals he was trained to watch for. At the first signs of her release, he climaxed in tandem, knowing his timing was perfect. Knew that even now her cervix was dipping repeatedly into his seed. The odds were good, better than the best they could do artificially, that she would become pregnant. Of course, it would take time to determine if the gender was right...

He lingered a few moments after her muscles stopped contracting. Keeping her legs elevated, he slipped a small pillow under her hips and stood up. Fingers gripped his thigh tightly as he moved to step away. Shocked, he glanced at the watchers, to see if they'd noticed, but her body partially blocked their view.

Her brown eyes were frantic behind her mask as her breathing grew steadily harsher. Her fingers released his thigh to reach along her side to where her pants still lay entwined around her ankles. A small plastic container lay just out of fingertip range. A frown creased his forehead. She was on drugs? A pleading glance came his way as she shifted minutely, but the container eluded her grasp. Her breath came in ragged gasps, but she didn't move from the pillow to get the object: a decision he wholeheartedly supported. They both knew just how important this was. Reaching out, he gingerly picked up the container and gave it to her, hiding his actions from the watchers as he did so. She pulled her mask aside and quickly slipped the opening in her mouth and inhaled.

He turned away, appalled. If this was the best they could do, their master plan had a serious flaw. He supposed she could have been the only one ovulating, but still...His mind raced with recrimination even as he meticulously cleaned and tucked his member away. He placed the cleaning cloths in the bag hanging over the door and grabbed a fresh set of gloves. The sound of the female's wheezing breaths made him turn back. He glared at her disapprovingly. Why had she been chosen? What were they thinking?

Despite his abhorrence, he watched, fascinated as she inserted the cartridge between her lips again. Her lips were fuller than his were. Round and soft. She caught him watching and mouthed the words 'thank you' behind her hand so they wouldn't see. Then her lips curved up at the corners. A smile. He was taken aback at the sight. Without a mask to hide the effect, smiling did something to her eyes. The small lines around them were more pronounced, but it also made them shine. The color became deeper, richer. He was used to watching the female's eyes for cues on how he should move, but nothing had prepared him for this. She sparkled. She glowed. Like the sun coming from behind the clouds... He shook his head at the foolish, poetic words that came to mind: a description of something he had never seen, but imagined for a lifetime.

Unbidden, his fingers reached out and stroked along the side of her face. Her skin was soft, like the powder lining his gloves. Her smile vanished, panic dancing across her features as she glanced at the two-way glass in panic. On cue, the door swung open and the watchers bustled inside.

The most matronly clucked at him reproachfully. "Into the shower with you. You know better. As if what you're doing isn't risky enough..."

His hand dropped quickly. Shocked at his own behavior, he backed away from the woman looking at him with something akin to terror.

"There now, off you go." The oldest women shooed him brusquely, placing herself between him and the woman on the cot. She hastened his departure by shifting her bulk insistently forward, forcing him to move backward to avoid physical contact. The door closed decisively the second he was clear.

He raised his hand to knock, to demand re-entry, but restrained himself. He would see her again this afternoon: the administration always made sure he had at least two sessions with an ovulating female, more if it could be arranged. Times were desperate. There were so few males left, and the ones from outside had few viable male sperm. He had been raised here, his environment as clean as they could make it. Every aspect of his life regimented: diet, exercise, sleep, intercourse. And he had almost risked contamination from a sickly female. Shaking his head at his own foolishness, he made his way to the sterilization chamber.

His mind was in turmoil. He alternated between fascinated obsession with the woman's face, the feel of her skin, and berating himself for not following procedure. Throughout it all, his body mechanically followed the sterilization protocol from long habit: clothes into the bag for sterilization, into the shower, wash from the top down with antibacterial soap. Cursing under his breath, he moved out from under the spray and opened a sealed package. After donning the sterile, close-fitting garments, he played with the string of his own mask irritably. It was starting to cut behind his ears again. He would have to say something about that.

The faint crinkling of plastic accompanied his every step as he walked through the compound. He found himself staring at the workers scurrying about their duties, wondering what they looked like beneath the impersonal protective suits. A few waved in passing and he attempted a smile in return even knowing they would not see it behind his mask. It had been a long time since he'd tried. It felt good.

The door to his room slid open as he approached and he removed the plastic booties before he stepping inside. The door slid into place behind him with a soft snick. He was home. All the surfaces gleamed, reflecting his muscular physique from all angles. Hearing the faint hum of the hepa-filters, he pushed aside his mask in relief. He would have to put it back on again when it was time to exercise, but for a few moments at least, his time was his own. He sank down on the bed and grabbed at the stack of well-worn magazines. A few loose pages fluttered to the floor and he leaned over to pick them up.

He shook his head in amusement, a real grin crossing his features as he stared at the familiar pictures. Gary would have something to say about all this; he always did. "Those ain't real women," he would insist time and time again. "They're pretty to look at, but not so good for breedin'." He'd flip through the pages absently, pointing out the flaws with a large, callused finger. "Too thin. Hips too narrow. Not worth your time." He'd toss the magazine to the floor in angry frustration. "At least they get that right here. Women need to be a proper weight, a little flesh on the bones, wide hips. Nothin' you'd see in there. Those ain't real."

Gary had been an old farmer when they still had such things. "Before they engineered all the chance out of everythin'," Gary would say with scorn in his soft voice. "Oh, no sir. There's no need to wait for rain, just feed all your plant the right mix o' chemicals and they'll turn out perfect." He spat derisively, wiping his chapped lips with the back of his hand.

"Them scientists, they know how to get the same tomato off each plant: none too sweet or too sour. They've got the answer for everythin', don't want to hear from nobody who works for a livin'. We saw what they were doin' with all their fancy chemicals before they did. It was workin' people who saw the crops wither and animals die. Long before their research would tell them, we knew they was poisoning everythin'."

"The government had us all stockpiling seeds to see us through when thin's went south. Got to save seeds for everythin'." Gary gave a shake of his shaggy gray head. He sat down on the edge of the thin mattress, his faded blue eyes warm. "That's what we're here for, boy. We've got the seeds. Got to save every one. Thought my time was behind me. Guess you're never too old to be a stud." He grinned a little ruefully as he patted his thickened midsection. "Course, they can't be too picky with the few of us that's left."

Damn. Sometimes he missed the old man and his observations. For the longest time they had lived together: two men adrift in the sea of estrogen. He let the magazine slip from his fingers as he lay back on the bed, one arm covering his eyes. The old man had seen what it was like out there, had lived through the worst of it, and survived. "Because I'm a tough ol' bird," he would crow proudly, his leathery features crinkled with mirth. When there was so much outside that could have killed him, it was ironic when the old man died in his sleep a few months ago.

A knock on his door had him automatically swinging his mask into place, although he didn't bother to sit up. He eyed the tasteless array of food with minimal enthusiasm as it passed through the UV filter. He dragged a spoon through the yellowish paste and let it fall back to the tray untouched.

"Those are not real eggs," Gary always insisted adamantly, disgust evident in his voice. "Nothin' like fresh eggs in the mornin'. They say we can't have the real thin' – too high in cholesterol. A little cholesterol is a good thin'. Keeps thin's a little stiffer," he added with a wink and a nudge, his eyes twinkling with mischief. "They say they just want us healthy. It's not healthy to deprive a man of some thin's." A long, suffering sigh. "Sometimes I just want a side of bacon. I bet if I got worked up enough, they'd get some for me. Bet if I didn't want to exercise, they wouldn't make me. They don't want to stress us out. That's bad for the count you know. That's all that really matters. We gotta be able to push those little Y's out."

Sometimes Gary's anger would erupt, and he would pace back and forth in the small confines of the room, his hair mussed and standing on end wildly as he muttered under his breath. "Not right for a man to be like this. Cooped up. Maybe you can do it." He acknowledged the younger man with a disconsolate slash of his eyes. "You've never been there. Blue skies, no one telling you when to start your day or what to do." His voice trailed off wistfully, eyes unfocused and staring as if some vignette from his past were playing out on the stark, white walls. His hand reached out, brushing over the unblemished surface before his fingernails compulsively scratched at the offending barrier sending small white flecks scattering over the polished tiles.

His hands stopped the movement abruptly as though suddenly aware of his actions. He turned around and bestowed a sad, knowing smile on the younger man. "This ain't bad for you yet, boy. I remember when I was your age. Not much I thought about beside the next pretty gal, but when you get like me, all you can think about is holdin' her, the one that means everythin' to you. You'll think about walkin' in the field, watchin' the sunset, seein' her smile." He choked on the words, his eyes soft and misty. "You'll know what I'm talkin' about someday. When this all gets to you, what you gonna do?"

Remembering Gary's words, he pushed the tray away and rifled through the magazine, trying to find a woman with the same lips as the female from this morning. Variations of female flesh stared up at him from the glossy pages; naked bodies sprawled in various positions, and he found himself echoing Gary's long standing arguments. He grinned as he tossed the magazine away, wondering how he'd turned into a cynical old man at 29.

He lay back on the bed and imagined what she would look like naked. She would be softer, rounder than the women in the magazine. He wondered what it would be like it she were free to respond to him, to touch him. What would it be like to have her skin touching his all over? The softness of her body, pushing against his. He shivered a little at the thought and shifted his member free from the rapidly confining cloth. Removing his gloves, he gripped tightly as if holding the images closer.

Knowing he should be focused on conserving his seed, he tried to restrain himself, but the images were too strong for him to ignore. He was tired of the quick, desperate acts completed solely to save the species. He wanted something more, something deeper, a real connection with another human being. Tension started to coil in his groin as he pictured himself touching her, taking the time to get to know what she really liked. What would it take to make her gasp with pleasure, to make her eyes go soft and darken to rich chocolate? But most of all, he pictured her smile.

A warm splash of liquid on his stomach heralded his release. Almost immediately several women burst in, frantically scooping up the seeds. Desperation drove their actions: who knew when the next boy would be born? He knew he should be helping. Hell, he shouldn't have done it in the first place, but all he could think about was the female with the chocolate eyes and warm smile.

Their rebukes were meaningless as he stared at the ceiling dazedly. He would see her again this afternoon. They had only a few short hours during ovulation and timing was everything. Maybe he would block the door and have the time to fulfill his fantasy. Just ignore the world and pretend it was just the two of them. He grinned at the thought.

"Be a sweetie," he drawled, interrupting the women's cackling tirade, "and get me some bacon."

Life and Death in the Backyard
Jill Koenigsdorf

The end of any year is a fitting time to take stock and reflect, and I have found that the best place to do this is situated in front of a large window that looks out into the wilds of ones backyard. It is my first winter here in Santa Fe, having moved here from The Bay Area in May, so I have seen the backyard go through only a few in its presumably impressive repertoire of transformations. Some people have jokingly summed up The Bay Area's change of seasons as simply: wet or dry, for once the rains begin in late October, they usually continue in their various forms: mist, deluge, sodden fog, or flood right on through February, greening the hills and making the use of one's clothesline out of the question. The up side of this is that hard freezes are extremely rare, so the growing season can seem endless. But the downside is: no brazen fall foliage, no icicles nor snow, no "earning" a case of spring fever once the long winter has ended and the days begin to lengthen and grow warmer.

Whenever I am in a new environment, one way I make myself feel more connected to it is to get to know the local flora and fauna. The High Desert, I have discovered, ain't no place for sissies. The plants outside my window are built for survival, not show, each on of them that is still standing in the dead of winter protected by some thorny cape or prickly armor. I recall stepping out into my garden after the night of the first frost and regarding the spectacle with shock and awe. It was as if some trickster was trying to antique my garden, waving a wand that instantly turned anything with a dash of color completely brown. Succulents drooped and looked gelatinous. The vines that had all season given me squash blossoms and so many Zucchinis, now lay limp on the surface of the vegetable bin like deflated black octopi. Pumpkin vines turned to mush. Even the volunteer sunflower, that last, late, sunny bloomer that sprang from under the bird feeder, bowed its head in defeat..

But now I face what winter throws my way less sentimentally. Out of my window, I see Aspen and Crabapple and Russian Olive in all their naked fortitude, bearing up against the howling winds and freezing nights, and I find their endurance inspiring. The wall of dense Wisteria, fondly referred to here as Hysteria, which once perfumed the back porch and sheltered us from those warmer but no less blustery winds in the long-ago evenings of summer, have lost every leaf and flower, their kinky frizz of beige looking like a giant disco wig someone tossed there then forgot. And those mysterious purple and green plants with the tiny flowers that once covered the vast expanse outside the Coyote fences, are uprooted now, showing their more familiar face: as Tumbleweeds, or, the aptly named, Wind Witch. Funny that this plant, an invasive from Russia, has become a sort of symbol for the Wild West, shots of it rolling across deserted and dusty roads gracing movie screens since John Wayne was knee-high to an Appaloosa. It is the ultimate desert survivor, scattering over two hundred and fifty THOUSAND seeds with every amble, garnering my respect, though on my early morning winter walks, crunching over the paths my own feet have made out back, I have to bend down every so often and fling the bristly orbs out of my way.

But it is the dramas occurring daily around the bird feeders that can really turn the backyard into one's own version of The Nature Channel. I have come to know the various feathered personalities that frequent the feeders: The Canyon Towhee is the big good-natured type, flying obliviously into open car windows or garage, brimming with social curiosity and happy to dive into the dog's water bowl for a brisk dip. The Robins who in other places symbolize the arrival of spring, but here seem ubiquitous throughout the cold months. The female Bluebirds, still gathering outside the nesting box we built, lining up to look inside, as if planning ahead for Spring. The house finches and chickadees picking out the choice morsels of seed from the feeders, letting the chaff fall to the ground for the accommodating Juncos. These icy mornings I start the day by boiling some water on the stove and heading outside to pour it over the frozen dome that was once the birdbath, wondering as I think of how important water is for everything in this climate, if birds can "drink" snow. The tiny forked footprints the birds have left in the new snow create interesting hieroglyphics as I make my way over to the small pond in order to break the ice with a sledgehammer we leave nearby.

When I am almost back inside I stop a moment, noticing how still the normally chirp and flutter filled yard is. Twenty feet from me, I see the reason for the sudden silence. A Red Tailed Hawk is perched on the fence, a sparrow dead and pinned under one set of talons, the hawk using its powerful beak to tug at its entrails as if they were strands of pasta. I watch his efficiency with a slight guilt, thinking maybe the songbirds I have drawn here are like sitting ducks for the lucky hawk, and also with the clinical fascination of a scientist. The hawk eats every scarp of the sparrow, including beak and feet and bone, then flies off to continue the daily tasks needed for survival. Within minutes all the birds come out of their hiding places and are again happily vying for the prized sunflower seeds at the feeders, life and death, kissing cousins.

The hawk makes me think about how we humans have a tendency to regard the various creatures on "our" property as good or bad. Even I in my efforts to be egalitarian, find myself rushing outside, crying "Shoo! Go Home!" armed with pinecones to throw when there's a standoff, when the Pinyon Jays arrive like swarms of locusts prepared to devour entire blocks of suet and several feeders of seed in a matter of moments. So I too have some wild kingdom rating system that says: Songbird=good; Jays=bad. The rats and scorpions and gophers and mice and yes, to some, even the coyotes, would fall into the "bad" category, while most people encourage butterfly or songbird. I recall when we were digging out back in the summer and a tarantula the size of a softball, striped and fuzzy, yellow and black like a bumblebee, made its dignified way to another part of the yard, to a rock that would not be so rudely disturbed. A rattlesnake too made an appearance on that backyard stage, dangerously near the hand that was reaching for the hose, the hiss of the water drowning out its own warning rattle. These two creatures were so novel that I didn't put them in the "bad" category, but actually felt sort of pleased that our backyard invited such variety.

And now as the mice skitter in the walls of the house, wreaking who knows what havoc to insulation and mortar, but to them, simply seeking a cozy place to wait out winter, I have to remind myself that there is an owl somewhere who might be very unhappy if we rid the planet of rodents. The shadows are lengthening and as the air cools, the drips spilling from the canales are once again reverting to icicle. A few birds are perched in the bare branches trying to catch the last rays of warmth from the sun. That stubborn frosting of snow clings week after week to the top of the picnic table, and I look at it anticipating the days when it will be warm enough to linger there, outdoors, again. During this year that brought so many changes, it has been instructive to witness the many progressions that this new place has to offer. And I have a birds-eye view for all that awaits me in the coming year, the unfolding dramas, the acquaintances ready to be made, both in the backyard and beyond.

Coming of Age in Chicago
Robert Lawrence

Saw horses barricade the street
for our annual block party.
Little kids frolic to the boom box
tethered to the neighbors' house
by a yucky orange extension cord.
Parents stand around and jabber;
the old folks sit and watch.
Oooo, and then the real action—
guess the number of jelly beans,
toss the colorful water balloons,
squeeze under the limbo pole—
leading up to the grand finale—
smokin' black-bellied barbecues
up and down the street:
hot dogs and burgers for all—
a real gourmet feast.

"Janie, all cooped up in your room—
turn down that music, will you—
come on and join us, and have some fun."
"I'm blowing this scene,"
I tell my mom. "Nothin here
but organized boredom;
you can reach me on my cell."
As I rush past her out the door
I smell her perfume—
eau de submission—
and resolve that her life
will not be my life.

Descent

Harmon Leete

The road of autumn, at its end
in failing light tips steeply
into the crypt of winter.
Unrelieved dark only can be seen
until its edge is lifted by St. Lucia.
Her smile and candle halo bright,
she leads us wonderfully
into a tent of festivals
as wide as sky
where blackness is a canvas to be painted
with all the lights of earth and heaven,
tiered chandeliers of stars and darting meteors,
gay storefronts, glowing windows strewn
across the white reflecting land,
channeling processions
of faces with red cheeks and laughing eyes,
torches and songs and horses' steaming coats,
camels, sleighs and shepherds, all on excited journeys
that merge here, in this hollow of the year,
in one great sharing blaze
that grows in brightness as we each emerge
rekindled luminaria
along the upward road.

Solar Power on the Prairie

Ellaraine Lockie

Here with the certainty that sun
climbs the Bear's Paw Mountains every morning
I return to the warmth each summer
Walk the prairie roads
when the sun's hands touch mountain's top

When they open perfume
on purple clover blossoms
Burnish pheasant feathers to a spit shine
And snap the stereo switch
that sets roosters and meadowlarks to music

A Chinook from the west
turns wheat into soft wind chimes
And cottonwood leaves
bend their ears into the whispers
While Cree ten miles east
talk to their God at this time every a. m.

The farmers rise and pray for rain clouds
to cry over dust depressed crops
But I welcome the hands of dawn
How they wander over my unbuttoned body
Strip the gray from daybreak
Stain my skin a kindle wood brown
Inject the fuel to burn for another year

The Beowulf Motel
Barb JoPresti

The floor seemed to absorb Daniel's feet like wet cement. His body flinched as empty whiskey bottles rolled off the bed and clattered onto the sleazy motel's filthy carpet. Feeling dizzy, he grabbed the night stand.

Where am I? He wondered, straining to see among the shadows. The sliver of moonlight filtering through the partially drawn curtains flickered as a figure passed the window.

Spotting the outline of an open bottle on the dresser and the Dear John letter his ex-wife, Jan had written over a year ago jogged his memory. Bitch. He licked his parched lips, picked up the bottle and drank like a man lost in the desert. Sucking down the last drop, he threw the bottle on the floor, where it clinked against a dozen others. The tattered letter sailed off the dresser, floated to the ground and landed at his feet. He dropped to his knees and sobbed as the words he'd read, at least a hundred times, echoed in his head.

> *Daniel,*
> *I feel like a coward not being able to tell you in person, but I can't take it anymore. After ten years I'm done pleading with you to go to rehab. And now, our little girl, the spitting image of you, mimics you by stumbling through the house, with one of your empty bottles in her hand. I'm done. My lawyer will be in touch.*
> *Jan.*

He wadded the paper into a ball and threw it across the room. Ignoring the poke in his stomach from his nagging bladder, he pulled himself up and sat slouched on the edge of the mattress, head cradled in his hands.

A brisk wind swept through the barren trees lining the property. The Beowulf Motel sign swayed on squeaky hinges; the only sound on a quiet night.

Daniel couldn't ignore the pressure of his aching bladder anymore. He staggered to the bathroom and flipped the light switch. The bright fluorescence stung his eyes, making him squint. He felt his way toward the toilet, swayed over it, missed and stumbled backwards as though a warm acid had soaked his feet. He reached for the sink to steady himself, and stared in the mirror. A gaunt, yellowed face stared back at him. He traced the dark circles under his hollow eyes with his finger tips then rubbed the stubble on his face and raked his fingers through his greasy brown hair. What have I done to myself?

Tears mixed with the snot running from his nose. Clenching his jaw, then his fist, he punched the pathetic reflection. The mirror cracked, distorting the image. Drops of blood dripped from his busted knuckles into the dirty white basin. Daniel's knees gave out and his eyes rolled back as his undernourished body fell to the floor like a dropped marionette. Before losing consciousness, he thought he'd felt a presence and something like ice cold hands against his flushed cheeks.

Daniel woke lying on the motel's lumpy mattress, staring at a multitude of water stains on the ceiling that looked like skeletal fingers descending down the wall towards him. He pulled the dingy sheets over his head and lay there cowering as he imagined the fingers reaching down to crush him. Finally, he lowered the covers wondering how he'd gotten into bed — maybe he'd been dreaming. From the corner of his eye he saw something move in the shadowy room. Then, he noticed the blood on his slashed knuckles. His brow tightened and a sudden chill seemed to paralyze him. A young woman stepped into the sliver of moonlight and stood at the foot of the bed. Her white skin was as smooth as porcelain. Red curly hair spilled over her shoulders, framing delicate features. She reminded him of a china doll and with the curiousness of a child he wanted to touch her. Instead, he recoiled against the head board. In the wink of an eye, she stood next to him. Gathering the covers to his chest, he gasped, "Are you an angel?"

She gazed at him with luminous green eyes. A slight smile crossed her face. "Is that what you think I am?" she asked.

He remained silent, noticing how her petite figure didn't cast a shadow. And how when she sat beside him the edge of the mattress didn't dip. Daniel drew back wondering if she was an illusion created by his fermented imagination.

"No. I'm real," she said, cupping his face in her cold hands, "My name is Layla."

His thoughts whirled. In a gruff voice, he stammered "Did, did you just read my mind?"

Leaning forward, she traced her thumb over his quivering lips, then closed her eyes and inhaled his scent as though it was an expensive perfume. He swooned, his head reeling.

"Let me take your pain and give you the life you've longed for," she said, in a voice smooth as ice. A knot tightened in his stomach. How did she know his deepest desire, one free of heartache and addiction. Adrenaline quickened his heart and his mouth went dry as he stared intently beyond the shadows in the room, contemplating her proposition.

Without warning, Layla grabbed his tangled hair, threw back his head and licked his jugular, pulsating under the tip of her tongue. She stabbed his flesh with razor sharp fangs. Daniel screamed and tried pushing her away, but she stuck to his neck like a gluttonous leech as she sucked his blood. Pain distorted his features, while his body shivered. Memories began flickering in his head like a silent movie. He saw himself at age nine, hiding under the rundown porch of his childhood home. Knees drawn tight against his chest, he listened for the snap of his drunken father's belt and the crunch of gravel under his heavy footsteps. Another image flashed showing Daniel in eighth grade, wearing black horned rim glasses and clothes too big for his scrawny frame. A group of girls were pointing and laughing at him. In an instant, he was transported to another time, his sophomore year of high school. He was sitting on his bedroom floor propped against the side of the bed, drinking a bottle of Jack Daniels.

AC/DC blared from his radio speakers, drowning out the rage of his inebriated father and the familiar sobs of his mother.

Layla withdrew her teeth, breaking the visions. Through a haze of confusion he watched as she inched backward on hands and knees, grazing her tongue over teeth smeared with his blood. His eyes fluttered closed, then reopened to reveal her kneeling at the foot of the bed, smiling like the Cheshire cat; a ring of red around her mouth like a cherry Kool Aid stain. The sight should have frightened him, but in his altered state the images of his past frightened him more. His thirst for alcohol began to rise and without hesitation, he accepted her proposal.

"You want this?"

He nodded. Laya hiked up her skirt, then slinked across the bed like a panther and straddled him. Daniel put his hands on her hips as lust surged through his weakened body. Then, she bit into her wrist and presented the oozing punctures like a gift. "Take. Drink."

Daniel hesitated then put his mouth over the torn flesh. At first the metallic flavor churned his stomach, then growing accustomed to its taste, he began suckling the wound like a new born baby at its mother's breast. Suddenly, memories not belonging to him flickered in his head. A hefty middle aged man with a vise like grip was dragging a little red haired girl toward a decaying wood shed. As her bloody legs scraped along the gravel road, tears streaked through the layer of dust coating her face. In an instant, the girl was a woman, sitting on the floor sobbing; a gold wedding band on her finger and a red welt rising on her cheek. A tall, thin man was standing over her with coldness in his eyes. Then, in a flash a male figure with iridescent white skin was slamming her up against a brick wall, biting her neck. Then with sharp teeth, he tore open his wrist and forced the bloody wound into her mouth.

Now, Layla's eyes fluttered and rolled back as she chewed franticly on her lower lip, "Enough," she yelled. Freeing herself from his grip, she darted into the shadows.

Like venom, her blood slithered through his veins striking his heart. His face contorted in pain while his body arched. "What's happening?" He shouted, frantically peddling his heels against the mattress and twining handfuls of tangled sheets in his fists. Then his heart stopped.

In death minutes passed in eerie silence before Daniel gasped, opened his eyes and slowly sat up. He knew something had changed. A pounding echoed in his ears. With vision as sharp as an eagle's he eyed the shadows. Layla stepped into the shimmering slice of moonlight and he realized the sound was the beating of her heart. A craving stirred, but it wasn't for the alcohol he smelled wafting from the bottles scattered on the floor.

Grinning, Layla stepped back. Her perverse peals of laughter echoed throughout the room. Like a blur, she vanished into the night.

He rushed to the window and threw open the curtains. But, she was gone. Standing in the moonlight spilling like a luminous ink over his pale, muscled body, he realized he was on his own. He gathered up his jeans, T-shirt, socks and shoes from the floor and swiftly put them on.

His hand held steady on the door knob, before he slowly opened it and stepped over the threshold into the night. Nature seemed to assault his awakened senses. The full radiance of the moon made him squint. Quickly, he covered his ears blocking out the deafening sound's of croaking tree frogs, the chirping symphony of insects and various critters rummaging through the foliage. His nose wrinkled against the pungent odor of the pine, spruce and cotton woods. Gradually, he grew accustomed to his heightened senses and began walking across the motel's parking lot; the black top like a conveyer belt beneath his feet.

What would Jan think of me now? Daniel wondered. Would little Megan even remember me? These questions plagued his mind until a pair of head lights cut through the haze of the early morning light, wrenching him from his thoughts. A car pulled into the lot and the driver side door opened. As a young woman stepped out, he titled his head catching the smell of cigarettes and cheap cologne. Her high heeled shoes clicked like castanets against the sidewalk as she hurried toward the building of the motel's office; an orange neon Vacancy's sign glowing dimly in the window. At first, he heard the raggedness of her breathing, but it was quickly drowned out by the pounding of her heart. A vile thirst awakened deep in his core. His mouth salivated. With the impulse of a wild animal, he stalked toward her.

As she opened the glass door and stepped into the office, the sun appeared over the tree tops like the head of an approaching giant. It burned his flesh as though someone had struck a match and was holding the flame against his exposed skin. He tried shielding his face in the crook of his arm, but the tissue began to blister and smoke. Torn between the painful scorching of the sun and his tormenting thirst, he frantically looked from his motel room, then back at the office door. It took everything inside of him not to scream. Then, realizing he might be incinerated if he didn't get out of the light, he dashed like a blur into the safety of his room.

Quickly, he closed the drapes, clambered over the bottles on the floor, crawled onto the bed and pulled the covers over him. He lay in a fetal position, vainly struggling to fill lungs that hadn't needed air since... What the hell did you do to me? he screamed in his head, thinking of Layla. Thoughts ricocheted in his head like a pinball when he realized... A look of horror contorted his face. The scream lodged in his throat as he burrowed soundlessly, deeper into the covers and he imagined oak barrels filled with human blood.

1

Voice of the Turtle

Alison Luterman

Day's beginning at the kitchen window:
mauve clouds, wind, another storm to the East,
the first bursting of pink peach blossoms.

Rain with its thousand soft drumbeats,
its habit of seeping,
its innumerable murmurous complaints
is falling dreamily into earth's cracks and fissures,
through rusted drainpipes,
on brindle mares standing in soaked fields with their colts beside them,
and on miserable hens which are not proverbial, but shivering.

The homeless man coughs his terrible cough
and shuffles along on swollen feet.
Rain falls on my mother's ashes,
long since washed to sea,
and on my friends lost to cancer, car accidents, and suicide,
on soldiers who did not return from the war.

This is how our dead come back to us
in the veiled, rusty sunrise,
in the cold trickle down the back of the neck,
clear drops falling on ducks hiding under tucked wings,
on the stroller-baby shielded in her make-shift plastic tent,
and the man pumping gas on a cement island, his collar turned up.
And this is how we will come back ourselves some day,
falling, splashing into the blushing center
and wet leaves of green-sheathed rosebuds,
into every open face passing by.

Those Who Swim with Wild Dolphins

Mary Makofske

Hour on hour they spin and dive
embraced by water, synchronizing
their movements with the dolphins'
until they swim beyond the physical
into an aquamarine of trance.
They swear time loses meaning,
fear drops away in the joy
of submersion, dance. Around them
dolphins glide and mate, chatter
and eye the curious intruders
streaking their portraits
through the water's colors, composing
a visual language with breath
that floats in quivering globes
to the surface. All they create
disappears, leaving no trace
an archeologist could follow.
Not only touch vibrates
with meaning; the spirals they weave
echo the helix where life began.
The swimmers drift far from the boat
till fatigue or cold forces them in.
Coming aboard again, they often weep.

Lessons in Waiting

Jessica Maynard

Snowdrops never seem to blossom quickly
in the spring. Lilies slumber,
in their tiny beds of earthworms.
Snapdragons refuse to roar, opting
for hibernation instead.
You're impatient, I get it. Wait.

Summer will be here, though this one will
be hotter than a Tepin pepper.
The sun, he'll follow you around,
your little sunny-buddy. You'll get tan first,
then he'll scorch your head, your arms,
your shoulders, 'til you can't
think anymore, 'til you can't wait for

fall. It's the season that's ever too short.
Jump into the red, orange, and yellow
sunset, and yellow, orange, and red leaves.
Do it before the whirlwind sweeps it all
away. Inhale that cool, musky,
breath of air, exhale

the blasted cold of winter. Ice will cling
to every oak branch, power line, and stand-alone
weed for a five-mile radius. You'll scrape
an arm, scrape a window. It sure is beautiful,
driving those miles down quiet country roads,
past the perfect, glittering, wedding-cake world.
You'll love winter, then despise winter.
Wait a little longer, then realize

the snowdrops never seem to blossom quite fast enough...

Spring Snow
Kathleen McElligott

Spring snow gently taunts, reminding me that tender shoots
wait patiently beneath the soggy earth.
Past my chin-high wall I glance
Through coveted windows. March flurries make me smile.

Plump flakes float earthward at their leisure,
ignoring the danger of a southerly breeze
A perfect blanket muffles silence; hiding city grime and sharp cinders.
These ancient cycles can't be rushed;
the pull of the moon, the change of seasons,
and endless pulse prevail despite mere mortals' schedules;

Nature's drama is its will

We can do nothing...but enjoy.

Butedale Rite

Karla Jinn Merrifield

When the ice thaws & the first floes
leave for their long passage down channel
all the ghost salmon return in a spring

ritual to the site where white water
falls into the cove & shadow of commerce
in the red flesh of their brethren falls

on their ghostly silver bodies, on all
the hollow memories of their lost species.
It is a celebration of demise—

not theirs – but that of the hungriest ones,
those alien creatures with machinery,
tin cans, solder, steam, a greedy streak,

a killing instinct, shamelessness.
The ghost salmon return to the shambles
& the silence, to the clean scents

of rotting wood & rusting steel,
the long, slow fade of human sanctimony.
The ghost salmon return & return & return

until a new tide turns, bringing
again their living kind from the sea
to this native place, their place on earth.

Wood Blues
Paul Miller

I first became enamored of blue-stain wood the moment I stepped into a vacant house for sale in a town along the northern reaches of Colorado. I was with Annie, who a year later would become my wife, and we'd decided that the apartment where we lived was becoming too claustrophobic. We needed a place to stretch out our lives.

We pulled up in front of a one-story clapboard house in the middle of the block. This place, built in 1929, felt different right away, with its centered door and wide front porch open to the neighborhood. The front room of the house especially captivated us with expansive windows facing three sides of the compass, flooding the room with light. The prize for me, though, was the east wall of the living room, which stood out like a shrine: Blue-stain pine paneling ranged from ceiling to floor, and I couldn't take my eyes off it. The lodgepole pine, cut a true three-quarters of an inch thick, was a deep, golden hue, with streaks of gray, tan, and blue running through the wood. The panels weren't perfect – a few of the tongue-and-groove joints didn't seat quite right – but still the blue-stain made the bare room inviting.

Standing in the living room, I knew this would be our new home. How could we lose, coming home to such warmth? The wood panels alone were the perfect embodiment of the way nature shows off its artistry. But then Annie started talking about how blue stain forms in the wood – she's a botanist, and takes care of the science while I indulge in esoterica – and I started having second thoughts about the purity and benevolence of nature. The fungi that colors the wood is usually spread by bark beetles. Though some purists think stain ruins the wood (one preventative measure calls for dousing green lumber in tetrachlorophenol before shipping), I couldn't stop looking at this lovely palette and seeing stories behind the complex hues, the life cycle of a pine coming to a close in some valley, a beetle carrying Ceratocystis spores into the wood and leaving a gallery of colors behind. I imagined the tree crashing to the ground in a windstorm, then draft horses pulling the log out of the forest. Sawyers with shavings in their beards would shape the wood, then send rough planks to market to produce finished wall panels. Such a bucolic scene, so far removed from the vast tracts of clearcuts that dot the planet like scabs – or the staggering number of beetles out there, munching their way through the woods, mindless and mute.

On this February day, though, logging and bugs weren't my primary concern. Within ten seconds of stepping into the house, we were imagining the rooms full of our books and chairs and friends. Weeks later, we signed the dense, scary contract and became homeowners for the first time.

Over the next 15 years, we filled the house at odd times with dust from renovations. Meanwhile, I ramped up my love affair with woodworking, hanging my tools on the straight walls of a garage I'd built.

I also continued struggling with the dilemma of how the wood turned up in my hands to begin with. Over the years, I'd seen the effects of what logging has done to the landscape, and I could no longer pretend the damage didn't matter. Walking down the aisle at a local warehouse, I'd see the logo of a lumber company stamped on a huge bundle of redwood or Douglas fir, and feel my face redden. How much old growth was sacrificed for this wood? How many species were displaced when a forest slope was clearcut? How many tons of sediments were choking streams from unchecked runoff?

And, face red, I'd pick up a few planks of wood anyway, because it wasn't much, and because I had a project to do. I figured that even the blue-stain pine on the wall of my home probably was logged in mountain valleys west of my home, and I wasn't about to atone for that sin. It had been cut before I was born.

I did manage to assuage my guilt by living more carefully. If I had to contribute to the felling of trees, then at least I could reduce my footprint on the planet elsewhere.

Not that long ago, life was much more lean, and conservation wasn't such a catch phrase. During a construction project on our home, we opened up an outside wall and discovered that the small back room had been added some years after the house had first been built. To help insulate the wall, pieces of cloth had been tamped into spaces at the end of the siding. Excavating further, we found more insulation: remnants of cardboard and newspaper tacked inside the wall. One small piece of newspaper pasted to stiff paperboard featured a cartoon from 1924 called "Harold Teen – The Sage and the Sheik."

The paper was being used as insulation. I loved the idea. As much as I considered myself a devout re-user, this old newspaper, as brown and fragile as ancient parchment, easily beat my best efforts. Like a time capsule, the newspaper spoke of an era long gone, when people used what they had and used it well until nothing was left. Careful conservation of resources has largely been lost to us, and we're poorer for it.

Standing in the shell of what would be a new room, I thought about how different our requirements are now, the two of us frenzied about adding a room in spite of our efforts to simplify.

"You know," Annie said to me later, reading my mood, "we're really not going overboard with our needs. We're making our home better so the next family won't have to worry about things like furnaces and pipes and where to put a new baby."

"Yeah, and nobody will have to go crazy laying down 50 feet of extension cord to plug in a lamp," I said. I was satisfied that our new addition had enough fiberglass insulation to keep us warm at temperatures cold enough to crack open trees.

But then, being true (and paradoxical) Americans in a land of excess, and because we seemed to be bumping into each other more and more in our small house, we eventually agreed we were out of room. Not all at once, but slowly, reluctantly, we finally decided to leave our home and the 800-some square feet that had sheltered us for 15 years.

We told ourselves that it was OK to expand our living space because we wouldn't be building a new home. Instead of chewing up resources constructing a place from the foundation up, we'd just look for what I cheerfully called a used home.

It would be hard to leave the beautiful, blue-stain pine in the living room, where landscape photos and family portraits hung. Whenever I opened the front door after being gone for weeks, the intricately veined pine was the first thing I saw. It was a gift, like coming home to warm flames in a fireplace.

We found a used home on the south side of town, a roomy place built in 1988 with light pouring into the rooms and easy access to bike trails. This would be the last, great place we would need, we told each other, clinking wine glasses in a toast.

After most of our home was settled, I set up woodworking equipment in the spacious garage, and, accompanied by chattering house finches in the blue spruce that lined the driveway, began building furniture for our new place.

I've come to accept that, no matter what I do, I'll leave a footprint on the landscape. Every home I've lived in was built of wood, but all that material, gathered from live trees, was put to good use providing shelter and warmth for generations of families. Where once I would cringe loading rough-milled lumber into my truck, I now vow to make the best possible use of the wood, to craft it into something aesthetic and useful that would last a long time.

I've also accepted that we humans aren't the only species to take what's needed from the land, leaving behind profound and sometimes irreversible changes. Vast stands of pine, some of which become stained with the array of color I like so well, are now being obliterated by the same tiny creatures that helped create the effect. Armies of bark beetles, western pine beetles, roundheaded pine beetles, mountain pine beetles – a few of the 6,000 or so species in the weevil family – chew into the trees to set up their homes, to reproduce, to move on to other conifers. What's left are ravaged neighborhoods of dead and dying trees.

Even healthy trees are no match for heavy infestations of beetles, something that happens in a lot of different places. In some areas, trees with no commercial value that are being destroyed may still have value to other life, but the bugs don't care. In Yellowstone, the mountain pine beetle is exterminating vast tracts of whitebark pines, the seeds of which are a major, seasonal food source for Clark's nutcrackers, red squirrels, and grizzlies. And with recent average increases in global temperatures, the beetles are feasting in places that once were too cold to support them.

So being human and needing to fuss over our planet, we argue about what to do. Let forests die, since it's part of the natural order? Cut ahead of infestations to create buffer zones? Set fires? Use noxious chemicals? I see this struggle between our own prolific human species and voracious bugs, and I think: What's better, who's more deserving? A chainsaw and lumberyard, or beetles and square miles of tasty trees? Who needs the wood more? Who will be here in ten thousand years to create beautiful blue-stain works of art?

I often think back to a moment I experienced years ago in the kitchen of our old home. I was gazing out the window, watching the wind blowing leaves into tiny whirlwinds in the narrow side yard. The sun was low in the west, and I could see dust and insects swirling around with the leaves, dancing in the late autumn heat. I became more and more entranced until, for an instant, I could see the house next door fall to pieces, the landscape absorbing all its contents over the course of thousands of years until nothing – until everything – was left, prairie grasses and shrubs and remnants of cottonwood leaves swirling in the wind. The world to the horizon was green and thriving, without a building in sight.

At that moment, I felt to my core that nothing we humans did, nothing we built, would change the decay and dust and rebirth that happens on unimaginable scales. Nothing within our grasp would make us see any clearer how geologic time reduces our best efforts to an infinitesimal shrug. My own shell, the carapace that allowed me to move around in self-made worlds, was rendered meaningless. I had been absorbed into the earth as easily as water playing on a forest floor.

For four months we owned two homes, but then we found good people who were anxious to buy our old place. We made a deal with the couple and wished them all the best. I had visions of them settling comfortably into the odd-shaped rooms and wandering around for weeks admiring our handiwork, bragging about how the former owners had left them with no repairs to make and almost nothing to improve.

I carried that notion with me when I stopped by to pick up our mail two days after the couple had moved in. From the sidewalk, I could hear hammering and loud voices and music coming from inside. Something didn't seem right.

I knocked on the front door. Through the screen, I could see a pile of lumber stacked haphazardly in the living room. Before fully realizing it, I knew what I was looking at.

The new owner came to the door, threw it open with bonhomie, invited me in. I stood transfixed. Mere hours after getting the house keys from us, he had torn off every last blue-stain pine board and tossed them all into an ignominious pile, a heap of pick-up sticks. Finishing nails stuck out of the wood like broken teeth.

I may have smiled, I don't know. I asked with a dry mouth what he intended to do with the wood.

"Dunno," he said, anxious to show me what else he'd been doing to the rest of our house. His house now, an impossible concept. "Probably haul it to the landfill. Want some of it?"

I stood frozen in what had once been my place of power, and stared at the naked wall, the indecently exposed wall, an ugly scar of decrepit plaster and lath. The man rattled on about how cool the living room would look after he was done, but I couldn't absorb any of it. Had I missed something all these years? Had other people visited and seen the tongue-and-groove as cheap and annoying, as some kitsch remnant from a bygone era? Could such warm wood have failed to touch the heart of this man, this young couple, so completely, as well meaning as they were?

But this was not my home any more, and he could rip the ceiling open to the sky if he wanted. At least I could salvage what he felt was useless. The landfill, sweet God in heaven.

"I'll be glad to take it off your hands," I finally managed. "Good thing I drove my truck over."

I spent a half-hour loading all the paneling into the truck, then scavenged around the living room looking for scraps, for any small slivers of wood. I felt like a forensic expert combing the scene of a crime.

A short time later I said good-bye, then drove slowly back to my new home, the wood behind me rattling like bones dancing a jig.

One wall of our basement is now covered in tongue-and-groove blue-stain pine, originally milled to an honest three-quarters of an inch thick.

Every cut I make in the wood – there's still some left – releases the haunting scent of antiquity, the countless years of trees standing against blistering winter winds. Particles of sun and rain, inscribed deeply in the grain, cover my arms in a dusting of light gold powder. Blue and gray veins, memorials of Ceratocystis spores, trace a meandering river of color, a map laid out in living fiber in a forest long since gone. Not a single one of us will ever know where that neighborhood once stood.

Chicory
Julie L. Moore

Chicory unfolds its petals like arms,
  blooming blue each sunrise in June,
  and looking at the fields, you could swear

the sky has capsized. But the story
  goes like this: Spurned by a blossoming girl,
  some surly, red-faced god turned her

into these weeds. So every day,
  as her roots grind past noon,
  as she tries in vain to cast off

the curse, if you close your eyes,
  breathe in the tight air,
  you can sense her periwinkle

pretense. So you won't be surprised
  when the world inverts,
  when afternoon sun forces

her bow, seals her in her own
  embrace. When the meadow
  clouds with Queen Anne's lace.

Perfectionist

Jylanne Musselman

During my neighborhood walk
my mind turned and whisked
   through cobbled thoughts in the sun,
searching for rhyme or reason, and flitting
   fast as hummingbirds to nectar.

I moved past sunflowers
who waved and bowed at me,
secretly wishing I were Van Gogh,
while monarchs applauded
their own ingeniousness.

I searched for seeds of inspiration
to grow a poem, dug deep for an idea
like Picasso's, wild and free.
I ignored Monet's gardens
dotting the landscape around me,
much like a painting by Seurat,
and in the process
   missed the point.

Amistad

(Excerpt from Harbor Boss: Confessions of a Chicago Public Servant)

Robert J. Nelson

Mid-morning on a dog day of August named for the dog star, Sirius, rising and setting faithfully with the waning summer sun: at Navy Pier I board the replica tall ship, Amistad. Stepping on deck of a square rigger is setting sail into the maritime past. The ship is a replica of the coastal schooners that plied the east coast, Caribbean, and Great Lakes 150 to 200 years ago. Smaller than most cargo ships of those times, these 100-foot schooners were fast, nimble, and more maneuverable in shallow waters, ideal for specialized (or illegal) cargoes.

She is an authentic replica of a famous slave ship with one exception: the cargo hold where slaves were shackled together in unbearable conditions has purposely not been replicated; it would be too shocking, especially for visiting school children. Instead the below-deck area is a mini-museum with artifacts and documents relating to the famous Amistad incident.*

Bill Pinkney, president of the Amistad America Foundation that had built the replica slave ship to take around the country to "encourage a conversation about race," called me last week and asked if the ship could come from its week-long display at Chicago's Navy Pier to the Hammond Marina for two days. "AT&T will pay all the docking and other costs," he said. Twelve years ago, Bill Pinkney, the only Afro-American to sail solo around the world was desperate for sponsorship and funds. He had a donated boat and a vision: to send live satellite feeds of his trip to black school children back in the states. Many thought he was crazy, but I thought his idea brilliant and for a couple of months allowed the boat to stay in a slip in Belmont Harbor until he found sponsors and provisions. When I reminded him that he was the only boater I ever gave a free slip in Chicago, he chuckled and added, "Those were good times, good times."

His circumnavigation was not only a historic achievement, but also an educational innovation that led to the building of the Amistad. When Bill asked if I wanted to sail her to Hammond from Navy Pier, where she had concluded a week of tours, I jumped at the chance.

We motor out from Navy Pier in a light westerly breeze, past the Monroe Harbor lighthouse into open water. The captain shuts off the auxiliary engine, one of a few modern addition to the ship, and orders the crew of eager college interns and a couple of old salts, to raise the sails. Braided hemp lines are pulled through dead eyes and wooden blocks. Slowly the sails climb the masts and unfurl from the cross bars. The breeze is light enough to carry full sail: gaff mainsail, mizzen mainsail, jib, staysail, tri sail, top gallant and mizzen top gallant. It takes the crew about 15 minutes to hoist them and tie off and coil the lines. As an American flag gently whips from the back of the mizzen, the heavy sled-like hull responds, heeling 10 degrees to port and south. The captain who has both hands on the massive wheel gives the crew orders to trim the sails. This seasoned sailor hired by the Amistad Foundation to pilot the ship around the country turns to me. "Sir, you know these waters. What's our best course to Hammond?"

I tell him to head for the water intake at 67th Street, then sight the power plant chimneys next to the Hammond marina and take that heading to Hammond. By taking those two angles, the ship will always be in deep water and away from the many sunken obstacles near shore. It is the same directions I have given hundreds of times to boaters coming to Hammond from Chicago.

"When in doubt, stay out," I tell him. He smiles in agreement, shifting his weight as the ship heels beneath a strong puff. The captain is middle aged with weathered skin, muscular hands and arms befitting an experienced mariner.

"Why don't you take the helm?" he says standing to one side of the cockpit, one hand still firmly on the wheel.

With both hands I step up and take the wheel, four feet in diameter, made of teak and highly varnished. The spoked handles are smooth and shaped like miniature baseball bats, the fat part extending out to keep hands from slipping off. Like all tall ships, the aft deck slants upward allowing the helmsman to see every part of the boat and rigging from the highest point at the stern. On tall ships, there are no enclosed bridges. Captains and crew are always exposed to weather and the higher steering position at the stern keeps the helmsman as far away as possible from storm waves crashing over the bow. For fair weather sailing Amistad sports a handsome wooden seat to break the monotony of standing behind the wheel for hours at a time.

Today's haze rolls down the hard edges of the skyscrapers like gray carpeting on stairs onto a darker gray lake. I turn the wheel slowly and the ship responds heading southeast toward the 67th Street water intake, a large structure built at the turn of the century from huge limestone blocks in 40 feet of water a couple of miles offshore. The intake, or "crib" as it is commonly called, looks like a castle or fort, perfectly round to deflect storm waves up to 20 feet from any direction.

After crew members trim the sails for a broad reach, Amistad begins to pick up speed. The ship's real captain takes a 360 degree look and then drops down the companionway below decks to make log entries. I am left alone at the wheel, virtual captain of a resurrected slave ship, sailing down Chicago's black south side, a coast with its own bloody history. Departing Navy Pier, we passed ironically less than one block from the trading post of Jean Baptiste DuSable, an African-American, the first known settler of the city in 1772.

Amistad glides past 31st Street beach, the 1919 site of bloody riots between Irish immigrants in established neighborhoods and black sharecroppers who had migrated to Chicago after World War I looking for jobs and better lives. Dozens of blacks were killed there. We sail on past the public housing projects at 35th Street, yellow brick high rise prisons built in the fifties, part of a "containment" policy for the growing black populations. From this distance out on the lake they appear small and confining like the "Barracoons"—the crude wood and iron bar enclosures on West African beaches where slaves were kept before the Middle Passage.

As we come within a hundred yards of the water intake I change course for the second leg to the harbor in Hammond about five miles away. At 71st Street, Rainbow Beach, named after a World War I highly decorated infantry division, became the frequent site of race riots in the fifties as white flight accelerated. A favorite beach of teenagers including me, it was closed frequently. Further south at 100th in Trumbull Park, a neighborhood of white, middle-class steel workers, more race riots occurred. One Sunday night in 1956 I was driving home from the Indiana Dunes with my then girlfriend, Kris, and another couple. We took a short cut through Trumbull Park only to be stopped by white thugs at a vigilante checkpoint near 103rd Street. With iron pipes and baseball bats they tapped on the windshield demanding to know, "Any niggers in there?" "None here," I assured them and even turned on the dome light to prove it. The racist thugs looked in and waved us along. Afterward I felt so ashamed

"I'll take her from here," the real captain says, patting me on the shoulder as he slips his hands onto the wheel spokes. Less than half-mile from Hammond he expertly heads her into the wind and barks orders to the crew. In a matter of minutes the sails are furled and all lines made fast. He turns on the engine once again as we approach the harbor entrance.

My plan was for Amistad to tie up on the end of "E" Dock which is close to the parking lot, office, and washrooms, but when the Captain sees the depth sounder flashing ten feet, nine feet, and then six feet as we approach, he throws the engine in reverse.

"We can't risk running aground. Let's dock somewhere else."

I try to assure him that my staff has checked the depth around "E" dock but he will not take the chance. Anything can happen on a wooden boat running aground. Planks can pop loose, keels and propellers can rip out, and masts can snap. So we hastily change plans and dock on the end of "V" dock where there is plenty of deep water. The problem is that "V" dock lies at the end of the main dock at the opposite end of the marina's public parking lot. Visitors will have to walk over a half a mile each way.

It is just past noon when we secure the ship and attach the boarding ramps. For the rest of the day black pilgrims gladly walk the half mile to Amistad. All day in hot sun they come, walking past a gauntlet of expensive white-hulled yachts on "V" dock to the black-hulled schooner at the very end. Once seized by slave mutineers, it is now seized by the imagination of all who come aboard. By the end of the next day, a thousand African-Americans, old and young, individuals, families, and couples, climb aboard and wait patiently in deep silence normally reserved for burial at sea. Almost all emerge from below decks in tears—once possessed as property, they are now possessed by memory and hope.

Amistad is a floating reliquary, like the silver chests containing bone fragments of martyred saints carried in wagons throughout Europe in the Middle Ages. Pilgrims traveled for miles to see the bones and vials of blood through windows of leaded glass. Amistad's portholes serve the same function. She is a vessel as holy as any carted around medieval cities of Europe, and that same sense of awe floods over these black pilgrims. Several times I walk with the crowds to the Amistad gangway giving directions and tour information. As they climb aboard to experience their unique collective memory, I stay on the dock off to one side out of the way and watch. Their faces become somber and their eyes abruptly turn away from mine. Perhaps, unconsciously, they are reliving the slave/master relationship, which forbade direct eye contact, denying any semblance of self identity.

Standing on a floating dock surrounded by pleasure boats, the trappings of that "pursuit of happiness" American dream, I feel a self-emptying of my own. Even with all my accomplishments in Hammond—a full marina, waiting lists, new buildings, a free and accessible sailing program, excellent staff, and all the other markers of success, I feel empty. In a peculiar way Amistad reminds me that public service is a form of indentured servitude—15 years of government service. The best job I have ever had increasingly feels confining and means less and less. Boredom fills my days and I look for any excuse to get out of my office. I am teetering on the line between hope and cynicism. I can barely deal with boaters anymore, listen to the pettiness of privilege, see the energy of success wasted on consumption, or tolerate the "where's mine?" attitude. No longer is the marina my parish, nor I its pastor. Any moral focus has faded to empty day dreams. I am so tired of public service—I want to escape from these 15 years of hard labor; to retire and move on to something else, guided by a moral north star. At least twice a week, summer and winter, I walk the marina beach and listen for voices, for the call of the sea again. I long to sail across another ocean as I sailed the Atlantic some 20 years ago, pause at the deepest point, and dive once again as deep as I can into the enormity of it all and then surface for fresh air.

At least twice a week, summer and winter, I walk the marina beach and listen for voices, for the call of the sea again. I long to sail across another ocean as I sailed the Atlantic some 20 years ago, pause at the deepest point, and dive once again as deep as I can into the enormity of it all and then surface for fresh air.

"Good-bye and fair winds," the captain of Amistad says, extending his hand to me over the rail of the ship. The docks that for two days were lined with black pilgrims are empty now as the sun sets behind Chicago's skyline. The crew pulls up the boarding ramp and prepares to leave. Amistad is bound for Muskegon, Michigan, a hundred nautical miles away to be there first thing in the morning for a two day stay, then north through the Great Lakes to the St. Lawrence and then the Atlantic. The engine cranks over and a puff of black smoke mixed with water spurts out the stern. Spring lines are uncleated and pulled aboard. The sleek schooner backs slowly away from the dock. I wave to the crew as they maneuver the ship through the harbor entrance. Once outside they raise full sail to harness what's left of the afternoon breeze.

I walk along the outer breakwater and watch Amistad, like a dream, become a black speck on the horizon. As it disappears I hear the lake rippling in whispers against the armor stones, telling me it is time to get rid of everything that won't fit into a duffle bag, sling it over my shoulder, and climb aboard.

*In 1839, 53 West Africans who were forcibly captured to become slaves, mutinied aboard the cargo schooner, La Amistad and took command of the vessel. After 63 days at sea, the ship was apprehended by the U.S. Coast Guard off Long Island and sailed to New London where the captives were jailed on charges of murdering the captain and crew. Hearing of the plight of the imprisoned Africans, members of New England Congregational churches took their case to court and ultimately the Supreme Court. The case took on historic proportions when former president, John Quincy Adams, argued on behalf of the captives before the Supreme Court: that they were African citizens and thus illegally kidnapped into slavery. Adams won the case. In 1841, the 35 surviving Africans were freed and returned to Africa. The incident is considered the first human rights case argued in the American judicial system, questioning the institution of slavery (Were they slaves and therefore property or not?) and testing the nation's founding principle that all people are created equal.

Spring on the Prairie—and in Vermont
Lynn Veach Sadler

I have lived on the prairie (well, Iowa and Illinois)—and in Vermont. In both, the winter snow mostly melts. The mud of the prairie dries quickly. Vermont mud is a fifth—full—season. I think of that claim awhile. I think of that claim a lot before crawling out from such of my secret places as Wherever, Brain; Wherever, Imagination; and Wherever, Heart.

While I'm thinking, grass begins to grow again on the prairie—and in Vermont. The prairie parades wild roses. Other prairie flowers prance. When horses and humans prance upon the prairie flowers, they shower the world in spring's delicate scent.

What did I smell in Vermont? That self-righteous, curled-in-upon-itself fern! You'd think it would be a Violinhead Fern. (It probably is in the rest of New England. To be sophisticated is often better than to be poetically apt. I think that's a New England adage.)

I probably think too often on such matters.

That Fiddlehead Fern, I'm thinking now. Did I smell or hear it? Well, I sure-Lord hear it now. Hear that Fiddlehead Fern! Every prairie state sings its own version of "Oklahoma." I don't think "Moonlight in Vermont" is the nth "Oklahoma." Vermont is not Oklahoma.

While I am thinking too much upon the audacity of that claim, a Fiddlehead Fern de-spirals and slaps me on the nose for want of smelling. I cycle back from the problem at nose to the problem at hand. Vermonters, I recall, dance that segue eagerly in emergent spring.

When Vermonters look upon the timid, verging shoots of spring, they rise, slowly, through minds' sludge, their spirits sucking after spring as if they are fish asphyxiating. The moose slogs more lightly. Cross bears clutch at sleep, finally emerging. At bear crossings, bears ballet, to Vermonters' wondering (and wandering) eyes.

Believe me, on the prairie, spring is sweet. In Vermont, spring is a miracle.

While you're pondering that delicate distinction, I'm retreating to e e cummings' "Just-spring," all "mud-luscious" and "puddle-wonderful." Unfortunately, it's all too "far and wee" from me. I ponder, finally remembering: cummings was from Massachusetts, not Vermont. Perhaps his Just-spring was not quite so far and wee. (And I'm not his "goat-footed balloonMan" either! Well, no man, surely, though I may have some of his hot air—but spring needs that in its struggle against winter.)

C'est la Vie. Quoi

Excerpt from unpublished novel: Little Deaths
Pacia Sallomi

It was a dreary summer day punctuated by an untrustworthy blue sky. I searched for an outdoor café with a quiet corner table. "Non." The waiter would not allow me to move the place setting to a different table. "Non. If you want only to drink, you must select a table without a place setting." He said as he replaced the placemat and silverware. He has determined which tables will be for non-eaters and they were randomly scattered about the patio.

"—Mais monsieur, I would merely like a bit of privacy. What difference—"

"Choisis une autre." He insisted as he waved his arms about. There was no compromising with the functionary's assumed power.

There are enough cafés in Paris that another was easily found on the pedestrian street near Les Halles. More perfect than the first—sheltered from the gentle but slightly cool breeze by a glass barrier on one side and the café behind. When the waiter discovered that I wasn't eating, he graciously cleared the table of place settings. I could order a beer, smoke as many cigarettes as necessary, make small drawings in my journal, random marks, randomly. No pressure. He would bring beer and not bother me again until I signaled for another.

I was sheltered under the mostly rolled-up awning so the awareness that it would soon rain was aesthetic more than pragmatic. Between beer number three and four, the blue sky turned a murky, sinister gray as clouds coalesced, as shadows swallowed light. Strong gusts of wind banged against the glass divider next to me. Thunder rolled in the distance. The waiter began to crank down the awning. The tables close to me filled. But the wind was insurmountable and it became evident that the awning could not be securely tied down to the flimsy glass wall. Two men held the unstable canopy and waved their free arms emphatically, "À l'intérieur—tous!" The French retreat.

Just as I settled on a bar stool in the corner by the front door, the glass next to my previous table shattered—cracking like high-pitched thunder. Tables and chairs began to slide across the street. Abandoned plates of food crashed to the pavement. The waiters folded in the awning and stacked tables and chairs helter-skelter against the door. It was 2:30 in the afternoon.

Rain didn't fall, but rather was thrown from the sky in thick sheets. As if a solar eclipse had suddenly materialized, the sky darkened to a grayish-blue-black. Pedestrians relinquished the streets. Lightening—quickly followed by thunder—cracked horizontally across the sky. Vibrated my bones. A man too large for his scooter slowly rode by turning sideways towards the café—his rosy round face grinning, his poncho soaked and sticking to his plump torso.

Ten minutes later... The rain stopped. The sun sliced through pieces of darkness. Couples reclaimed the streets. Inside, conversations revived. Free coffee was poured. The waiter's drenched shirt was already drying in the breeze as he rearranged the tables and chairs linearly. The broken dishes were swept up. Pigeons pecked at the scattered pieces of bread.

The storm had passed.

Customers once again took their places at the outdoor tables.

This had nothing to do with hope.

C'est la vie, quoi

1

Welcome to New Hope
Paul Saluk

The small town grew
as US1 merged with Main Street.

An oasis for travelers
it nourished the needs of the tired and weary
and flourished on hard-earned prosperity.
                                        Until
the new Interstate swallowed
the tourists and turned time around.
                                        Today near Main Street
kudzu, not children,
twist and turn in the school house,

dry rot and bramble climb fences
where bougainvillea once flourished,

shops with doors that hang
on one hinge
creak in the breeze,

the cemetery sprouts
patches of weeds
that outnumber the dead,

the bank
that echoes once-held dreams.

Young Grandpa in Brooklyn: First Sunday

Arthur Schwartz

Suddenly awake, the Zayde listens prudently
to noise outside, and makes a judgment:
all this clamor is, for now, demanding nothing.

It's early; he stays still, listening to hooves
that clatter, voices, trains that shake the bed,
and still there is no need for a response, and

Calmed he calculates the distance he has traveled,
counts the borders, sees the great ship Rotterdam,
compares two names, the first no longer his,

And hears his wife, the grandma's urgent voice, and
sees them leaving, sees his little daughter's face
when they are stopped for questioning at Vilna,

Thinks of the neighbor who first told about
this place, imagines famous Washington,
whose high ambition was for streets like this;

Then, cautiously considering new strategies
against these sounds that are no more than waves
that lull and gently rock, and lying back,

He mulls the chance of sleeping late amazed,
and answers yes aloud, and closes tired eyes with
gratitude for Washington who wished this neighborhood.

Replenished
Lynne Shapiro

A windless freeze
sets the lake early this year,
black ice.

Stare down hard
into this watery clearing
and see all the way to springtime:

leaves become trees that sway,
fish crouch in their bones awaiting
the iridescent thaw,
pollen, roe, and eggs hatch into
raucous food.

I watch my husband and son skate
in and out of another winter,
their itineraries marked in scrapings,
accompanied by croaking ice
and the shadow of crows.

Everything lives forever
in nature's palimpsest:
Thaw replaces thaw; bird,
bird; fossil, fossil.

Pangaea*
Susan Baller-Shepard

He comes in unannounced.
I want to be alone, silent
sunk down in a tub with water
hot as I can stand.
"Mommy, this is your land!"
He says, puts plastic planes
on the brown islands of my thighs
and the plateau of my chest.
"You be land—don't move."
Dinosaurs perch near my collarbone sandbars
his pajama sleeves drenched
as he peers over the basin's rim
to plant toys on Pangaea,
Mother Continent.

Laurasia* and Gondwana*,
my sons will shift and slide away,
oceans will form between us,
all that was easy and within reach
will not be in the future.

I remain still. I hold my pose.
I am land and earth and ground.
Then his brother calls, "I think
the frog got loose," and he is gone
dripping out the door. I slip under
water, everything floats off me.

* The Pangaea theory states that all present continents were once together collectively known as a 'supercontinent' called a Pangaea during the Mesozoic Era. Laurasia: a hypothetical continent that (according to plate tectonic theory) broke up early in the Jurassic Period (approximately 200 million to 140 million years ago) becoming North America, Europe and Asia. Gondwana: Hypothetical former supercontinent in the Southern Hemisphere, which included modern South America, Africa, southern Europe, India, Australia, and much of the Middle East and Antarctica.

Back on the Hillside: of Strawberries, Chickadees & Memories
Bill Sherwonit

Summer, 2007. The July rain has eased into a drizzle, but heavy clouds still drape Anchorage's Hillside as I pull into a driveway off Soldotna Drive, bound for a homecoming of sorts.

I lived here for nearly 13 years, before the end of a marriage led me to the city's Turnagain area last fall. I hauled away most of my belongings months ago, but some stuff remains: assorted outdoors gear, a pile of clothes that will become giveaways, files and drafts from my writing life that I haven't needed, personal journals that have been buried for years, and tall stacks of magazines destined for the recycling center.

After a series of delays and projects to make the place more appealing, the house that Dulcy and I once shared is finally on the market, so it's time to finish the cleaning-out process. I'll start with what's in the garage, then rummage through the storage shed out back.

Entering the driveway, I notice the flyers that accompany the "For Sale" sign. I grab one, curious to see what makes my former residence an attractive buy, at least from a real-estate agent's perspective. "Decks Galore in Woodsy Setting," the flyer proclaims. Below some photos and the price, 10 bulleted items give more details. Those include the house's four bedrooms, its hot tub "with commanding view," outside sauna, shop plus storage room, private setting, and more.

There's no mention of what I found to be most delightful about this place, except for one brief mention: creek. That would be the South Fork of Little Campbell Creek, whose rushing music I remember as a soothing tonic on some stressful days. The "woodsy setting" offers a hint, of course, but it doesn't really capture the magic of this "499 sq. ft. MOA Lot."

The spruce-birch forest here is seasonal or year-round home—or in some instances, a travel corridor—to all sorts of birds and mammals. While living here, I saw and/or heard more than 40 species of birds, from the black-capped chickadees that expanded my sense of the world back in 1993, to the sharp-shinned hawks that took down a junco in our front yard one summer and a pine grosbeak the backyard another winter – and those were only what I witnessed.

Dulcy and I also observed 10 species of mammals, from the tiny shrews that tunneled through snow drifts beneath our backyard decks; chattering, seed-stealing squirrel; the cow moose that rested on the lawn with her two newborn calves; and the black bears that passed through like moving forest shadows.

More delights. Each spring and summer our "woodsy setting" gives rise to bunches of beautiful wildflowers. And from our upper deck's "commanding view," 20,320-foot Denali, "The High One," can be seen peeking between the spruce treetops, gracing the northern horizon. No small thing, that.

No mention of the weather, either, though that was certainly a major part of our time here. But I suppose you don't want to promote longer winters and deeper snows than those experienced on Anchorage's flats.

Getting out of my aging Toyota, I notice another piece of what made this place so special to me: the small patch of feral strawberries I annually tended and harvested.

I had originally planned to haul a few of the plants away and replant them at my new home, a one-story rental near the Coastal Trail. But during the move I gave up that idea, thinking it easier to leave my strawberry passion behind.

Now, in a flash, the passion is rekindled. The garden is bursting with dozens of large and luscious red fruits. I used to take some pride in my tending of this small garden. It was my patch and I faithfully weeded and watered it and harvested the berries, usually enough for a couple of pies. But this year's crop is richer than any I can remember. More berries and bigger berries. Many of them are huge by my patch's standard.

I'm humbled and excited. And just a bit chagrined. The abundance of flowering clover, grass, and assorted other invaders—including the start of a birch—makes it clear that neither Dulcy nor anyone else has been tending the patch. I can only guess that lots of May-June sunshine, combined with midsummer's abundance of rain, is responsible, perhaps assisted by benign neglect. Could I have overworked the patch? No matter now. All that's important is that no one has tended the plot or begun picking berries.

Dulcy has been traveling for more than a week, so she may not even know how well the strawberries are doing. And she won't return for several more days, so without any guilt whatsoever, I decide to pick a bunch before I depart.

Leaving the patch, I enter the house. Accompanied by years of memories and, yes, some nostalgia, I visit several rooms to see how Dulcy has arranged them for prospective buyers. A few of my photographs and pieces of artwork still decorate the walls and they'll remain until after the house is sold.

My tour complete, I step inside the garage and push the button that opens its door. Settling in, I spend the next couple of hours emptying shelves, tossing unwanted stuff into garbage bags, and piling magazines and boxes of files into my car. After a run to my storage unit and the recycling center, I return for a second load. It's peculiar that things once considered memorable and important to save can so easily become junk. That, I suppose, is one of the benefits of moving, especially to a smaller place.

With my car filled a second time, I sweep the garage floor and check to see if I've missed anything important. I've left behind a few things whose ownership I'm not sure about. I can always get them later.

Back in the kitchen, I reach inside a cupboard and grab two plastic containers. Then, once more outside, I kneel down and begin picking. And eating. The pinkish fruits are every bit as sweet as I remember. Again I'm struck by how fat and healthy they appear. There are no signs that any have been chewed on by bugs or birds or moose (a cow and her calves once invaded my plot). And no slugs are apparent, despite recent wet weather.

Taking a look around, I notice that the lawn, too, seems to be in exceptionally fine shape. I can't imagine that Dulcy has used any sort of pesticide on the yard. Still, I know she's hated the dandelions and other weeds for years and more than once wondered why I simply pulled them (or plucked their heads), a losing battle for sure. Maybe I should wash the berries when I get home, just to be safe.

While picking, I revel in the chattery songs of black-capped and boreal chickadees and their common companions, red-breasted nuthatches. I noticed the birds' bright, energetic voices soon after arriving, but their avian chorus has expanded and grown louder. It seems likely that recently fledged birds are joining their parents in talk and song.

Instinctively, I whistle back to the birds. While living here, I frequently whistled to the chickadees and nuthatches while putting out seeds, watching them feed, or working in the yard. Now I wonder if any might recognize my voice. Could it stir some faint memory in them?

Surely it's folly to hope that they might take some pleasure in my whistled response to their songs. Yet I must admit to such an odd longing. What really matters is that the birds' loud vocal presence in and around the yard on this gray and subdued afternoon cheer me no end.

My picking of the ripe fruits done, I head to the backyard. Walking across the lawn, serenaded by chickadees and creek water and refreshed by the lovely purples and lavenders of monkshood and wild geranium, I'm reminded that the yard and this neighborhood's wild inhabitants, more than the house and its interior, are what made this place special to me. I hope the folks who buy this place experience the "woodsy setting" as more than a scenic backdrop for their lives. I hope they pay attention to the other life forms that reside here.

Returned to the driveway, I prepare to leave. I still haven't gotten my things from the storage shed. But that gives me an excuse to return later in the week, when more berries will have ripened. I think I'll bring a pot or other container, because transplanting some of the strawberries once again seems like a deliciously wonderful idea.

Harbingers of the Next Century
Wade Sikorski

It's spring, and it is springing the way it usually does in southeastern Montana—an all-too short moment of green relief from the winter's cold trials of wind and snow before the onset of summer's relentless tanned landscape. I find myself out, going around the fence after the spring planting is done on my family's ranch. I like fencing. It is an opportunity to be by myself, alone with my thoughts. I love the fresh smell of grass emerging over the musky smell of decaying grass that the winter's snow pressed flat on the ground. I love watching the wary antics of rabbits as they eye hawks swirling overhead. But the last couple of years, my thoughts have taken a more troubling turn.

Spring fencing is an opportunity to take note of the changes time brings with it. Some changes have had their moment and returned again, like a corner post that I made in my youth. I'd assured myself would last forever, but discover it needs replacement again. Other changes are completely new, like seeing how cheat grass has climbed up to the top of our buttes, where only native grass grew before, or seeing a species of bird that I have never seen before, singing a song I've never heard before.

As I follow the fence line, I am carried even further back in time to when perhaps my great grandfather, or more likely, my grandfather, my granduncles, or a forgotten hired man did as I am doing. The fence line has seen many fencers come and go. Next year, 2011, my family will celebrate our 100 year anniversary of living on this place. And so, as I repair a splice so old parts of it are welded together with rust, I check my fencing skills against previous efforts, the kind of splice they made, the number of turns, their diligence, or lack of it. The wire in my hands goes back to the time when my family still used horses to work the fields and pull wagons, and when steam tractors were the advancing technology. Made much like the locomotives used to pull trains, these behemoths wandered the hills of our place like dinosaurs, breathing fire and smoke. Steel wheels, perhaps 10 feet in diameter, and a couple of feet wide, provided the traction need to pull the plows that broke up the prairie. Various pieces of them lie discarded along the fence, a strange assortment of broken gears, bent shafts, and twisted bits of metal that someone didn't bother to carry back home to the junk yard.

In those days, cedar posts were often used to make corner posts. Gnarly with age, weathered by wind and rain, and covered with mold and lichen, they often are leaning, as if rotted out. But I know that if I pull them out of the ground, and scrape the dirt away, the wood will look as fresh as the day they were buried. Instead of making a corner post that looks like an H, as my father taught me to do when I was a child, the people who put them in usually braced them diagonally, going from the top of the post down to the ground four feet away. Even though the cedar posts haven't rotted, the pull of the wire over the decades has been slowly, perhaps a hair's breadth a year, levering them out of the ground, leaving them barely anchored. Too often, I find myself replacing them with new corner posts that won't last a faction of the time, erasing the mistakes of the past.

In a draw where the snow laid deep during the winter, burying the steel fence posts that used to hold up the barbed wire, there is the evidence of the much more regrettable mistakes of our present that increasingly troubles me. For an entire stretch about a hundred yards long, the weight of the snow resting on the wires as it melted, has forced the steel fence posts deep into the soft spring ground like a straw settling into a milkshake. The steel fence posts should be chest high, an impassable barrier to an animal that is never more than chest high. Now the tops of the posts only reach my knees. If the cows could survey the fence in its sad state of repair, I'm sure they would leap over it, kicking up their heels, as if saying, "Free at last, free at last..."

This, obviously, will never do. I stop the pickup, pull on my gloves, and reach for the fence post puller. The puller has made my work much easier the last couple of years. It is just two tubes of steel, a fulcrum and a lever that has a clasp on the end of the lever to grab hold of the post. I go to the first post in the line, and put the base next to the post, raise the lever up, settle the clasp around the post, and ratchet the post up out of the ground. It is all so easy. At a restaurant in town one Sunday, I ran into a neighbor who had also recently bought one of these tools as well. We marveled at its simple engineering. We shake our heads and wonder, what had we done before?

Then it occurs to me: we hadn't really needed anything like this tool before. We didn't use to have to jack long lines of posts out of the ground in the spring. When I was a child, the wire would break from the weight of the melting snow, but the steel posts would stay where they were. Still frozen, the ground held the posts firmly in place as the snow melted. However, for the last decade or so, the frost has been out of the ground when the spring blizzards came. Now, when the snow melts, the ground is soft mud, unable to hold the posts in place, and so they sink.

For a while now, I have been contemplating the meaning of this change in my annual spring routine, having to pull posts back up out of the ground. It is a small change, to be sure, and I would hesitate to complain about it—if it were not a harbinger of so much more.

On another part of our ranch, we have a draw filled with trees. My family has long treasured them because most of southeastern Montana is treeless. Recently, we discovered that the trees are all aging, near death, and no new trees are replacing them. Alarmed, we invited a government scientist in order to try to figure out what was wrong. He speculated that a shift in grazing patterns had changed everything. The buffalo used to concentrate their grazing on the prairie, tearing up the ground with their hooves, leaving the ground trampled and bare, perhaps giving tree seeds a chance to get started. To see if this explained what was happening, he had us fence in two test plots on the draw. One we grazed heavily with cattle, the other we didn't graze at all. However, after a couple of years passed, it was clear that concentrated grazing didn't change anything. No new trees were starting in either plot. After some reflection, the scientist told us that he believes that the reason the trees are not reproducing in our draw is a change in the hydrological cycle due to climate change.

It's the same problem as with the steel posts. The warmer winters are melting snow throughout the winter. Snow does not accumulate on the ground the way that it used to, piling up deep in the draws where the trees are. Without the heavy snow to water the tree sprouts and to delay the grass, the trees are finding it too hard to compete against the aggressive prairie grasses.

Other changes on our place suggest more serious economic consequences. On our ranch, we have a flood irrigation system of about 60 acres. When I was a child, the spring melt usually filled the system of dikes with runoff from top to bottom. Some years, we might even have had two or three times as much water as we needed to flood all the dikes. One of my most vivid childhood memories is standing on a muddy dike in the middle of this project, water all around me like a sea. Cold, wet, and tired, I had been dragging ten pounds of mud on each boot around all day, walking up and down the dikes to open and close the watergates in the dikes. Little more than three feet tall, if I slipped on the mud and fell I would have been in over my head on either side. I didn't know how to swim, and doubted if I could anyway with my winter clothes on, so my thoughts were tending toward rebellion.

Today, cold, wet, and tired isn't a problem because the water doesn't come anymore. For the last decade or so, I could walk the lands between the dikes most years and not even get my boots wet. Perhaps our annual precipitation has declined, but not by that much. What has happened is that our long cold winters, where the snow accumulated until spring and then melted in a rush, have changed. Now the snow typically melts away throughout the winter, frequently leaving the ground bare, without snow cover. Without the white snow to reflect the sun, the dark ground absorbs more heat. By spring, the ground has thawed and the water soaks in before it has a chance to run off into our irrigation project.

This irrigation system, which worked really well throughout my childhood, is not watering our land anymore. As a result, the hay windrows that used to be too big for me to jump across, are now only a casual step wide. We used to get more than enough hay off this one piece of irrigated ground to feed our cattle herd all winter long. Now we hay a lot more ground to do the same thing.

※※:※※:※※

According to a recent federal government report, Montana will average 50, maybe even 60, days a year with temperatures over 100 degrees by the end of the century under a high greenhouse gas emissions scenario.1 On average, temperatures across Montana could increase more than 10° F.[2] This report might be conservative. A recent study by the Massachusetts Institute of Technology called "Greenhouse Gamble" shows that under both a "no policy" scenario, which is to say business as usual, and a scenario where nations started to take some action in the next few years, the odds have shifted in favor of larger temperature increases than has been previously reported. By the end of the century, there is a 1 in 11 chance that the global average surface temperature will increase by more than 12.6° F. There is a 90% chance that the increase will be between 6.3 and 13.3° F.[3]

People who are not farmers might not understand what this means. An increase of something like 10° F in Montana—which, by the way, will be less than most of the rest of the United States—would radically decrease the productivity of my family's farm. Several times, especially during the droughts of the late '80's, our fields looked lush and green in the morning. The leaves provided a canopy over the ground, choking out the weeds and protecting the soil from drying out, promising at least a decent harvest despite the drought. Later that day, after the temperature went over 100, the crop had clearly deteriorated. Bare ground was showing through the canopy because the leaves had narrowed, withered, and shrank. It was as if, like a turtle, the wheat had pulled its stems and leaves back into the ground, trying to keep itself safe from the harsh sun.

My rule of thumb, which is probably conservative, is that for every day temperatures are over 100 degrees, our wheat yields fall one bushel per acre, two if there is a dry breeze. Using no-till continuous cropping, the spring wheat yields on our place are now between 20 and 30 bushels per acre. If we assume that only half of those 50 days over 100 degrees will be during the growing season, our yields will fall 25 bushels per acre with the higher temperatures. In other words, my family might not even be getting our seed back by the end of the century.

Scientists are only slightly less gloomy than I am on the impact of higher temperatures on crop yields. Crop ecologists believe that for every 1.8° F rise in temperature above historical norms, grain production will drop 10 percent.4 Similarly, a paper by Wolfram Schlenker and Michael J. Roberts reports that corn yields across the United States could fall by up to 80 percent under a high emission scenario by the end of the century.5 Yields like this simply won't come close to feeding the world's growing population. People will starve, possibly by the billions.

For a century, my family has endured blizzards and droughts, and we have survived plagues of grasshoppers, bankers, lawyers, and low commodity prices. The natural disasters were bad, but to my way of thinking the human-caused disasters, the ones that typically involved politicians, bankers, and lawyers, were always worse. Over the next century, we are going to confront them together, a human-caused natural disaster. The harbingers of that future are already upon us. We simply must not, must not, allow the worst to happen.

1 Global Climate Change Impacts in the United States, Thomas R. Karl, Jerry M. Melillo, and Thomas C. Peterson (eds.), (Cambridge: Cambridge University Press, 2009), pp 90. http://www.globalchange.gov/usimpacts.

2 Global Climate Change Impacts in the United States, pp. 29.

3 Sokolov, A.P., P.H. Stone, C.E. Forest, R.G. Prinn, M.C. Sarofim, M. Webster, S. Paltsev, C.A. Schlosser, D. Kicklighter, S. Dutkiewicz, J. Reilly, C. Wang, B. Felzer, J. Melillo, H.D. Jacoby, "Probabilistic Forecast for 21st Century Climate Based on Uncertainties in Emissions (without Policy) and Climate Parameters," Journal of Climate, 22(19): 5175-5204, 2009, http://globalchange.mit.edu/resources/gamble/.

4 Lester R Brown, World Grain Stocks Fall to 57 Days of Consumption, Earth Policy Institute, (June. 2006) http://www.earth-policy.org/Indicators/Grain/2006.htm.

5 Wolfram Schlenker and Michael J. Roberts. "Nonlinear temperature effects indicate severe damages to U.S. crop yields under climate change," Proceedings of the National Academy of Sciences, 106 (37), September 15 2009, pp.15594-15598.

Counterfeit Face
Grazina Smith

A mottled purple bruise, too large to hide with sunglasses, slithers down over my left eye and covers half my face when I fly into Jackson Hole, Wyoming in August. The doctor has removed seventeen stitches from my forehead. It doesn't hurt and could be forgotten except when people near me glance up and bug out their eyes. I hide the bruise on the plane by tucking my left side against the window but in Jackson, every waitress, every store clerk, every woman passing me, gasps and clamps her lips into a tight line. If I'm alone, they often sidle up to me and whisper: "Are you all right?"

"Yeah, I...I walked into a door," I stammer, looking down, and then quickly peer over my shoulder to see if Paul was nearby. He doesn't notice what I'm doing, but the women never miss that surreptitious glance. If Paul strolls toward me, their gimlet eyes turn to ice and rake him up and down. It isn't hard to imagine what they're thinking and what they see. Paul was still not bad looking: tall, thickening a bit around the middle, he ambles with a loose-jointed grace. Usually, there's a boyish, "aw-shucks," grin on his face and I can tell when he is nervous by the way he constantly strokes his crew cut as if checking how much hair's left up there. I can read his actions better than he can read mine.

We're in Wyoming to join an archeological dig in the southwestern part of the state. This is our third summer volunteering and I wasn't very eager to go. Paul decided we should spend a few days in Jackson Hole as tourists and I spent the time trying to figure out how to avoid the dig. It is in the middle of nowhere with the hot sun beating down and a constant wind stirring clouds of dust that cover everyone. The work is tedious, days spent hunched over a pile of dirt, scraping to find some tiny, meaningless dinosaur bone. We spend the evenings with Paul's "colleagues," and after dinner, they preen as they drink their scotch on the rocks. When they total their yearly accomplishments, Paul clearly is out of their league. He's still an adjunct professor, never full-time for even a year, never published many papers and never a speaker at a symposium. I think the group keeps inviting him back because he makes them look so good and, deep down, I think he knows it.

Paul is a long-winded, stubborn man. He's always trying to mold me by telling me what books to read, what music is best, what opinions to have, how to do things and nagging me if I don't agree. He never raises his voice but drones on like a fly against a window pane until he wears me down and I accept his "expert" views. Our life together feels as if I've stepped through the looking-glass into a topsy-turvy world and, just to get some peace, by supper I reconcile myself to the things I didn't believe at breakfast. I'd dropped out of college after my sophomore year, partially from lack of funds but mainly from lack of interest. I still read a lot, but Paul has a number of advanced degrees which he never fails to allude to during his interminable lectures. However, having masters' degrees in the study of medieval English architecture and in ancient Sumerian languages doesn't bring home the bacon.

Every once in a while, I say to my sister, "Paul is such a bore. Sometimes I feel I need to get away from him."

She's always horrified: "but you were lucky to make such a good marriage..." she begins. "You just don't know what you want." In a way, she's right but I do know that, this year, I don't want to spend any time at this dig.

"Did you see how people gape at my bruise?" I ask Paul. It's not the sort of thing he notices but now he stares at the women who give him long, hard looks and the men who avert their eyes. "The guys at the dig will give me a really hard time," I sigh. Paul only grunts, but realizes he will be the butt of all the jokes that mask unspoken accusations.

A day later, Paul asks me. "Would you rather spend the next three weeks in a cabin at Yellowstone? The doctor said a lot of sunlight is bad for the scar on your forehead." The doctor actually said I should slather it with sunscreen but I don't remind him. With a shrug, I answer, "It might be a good idea."

Paul spends the next day and a half looking for a place for me to stay. It's late in the season and everything we can afford is booked. He's taking the rental car with him so I can't stay anywhere very remote. Hope is running out, but when I come back from a walk, he's beaming.

"There's a room available at Colter Bay Village in the Grand Tetons." He says as his hand massages his crew cut. "It's on Lake Jackson and there's a marina, hiking trails, a restaurant and a gift shop."

"It sounds good."

"The room is in the guest registration cabin, off to one side of the desk. They don't usually rent it, but I told them we were desperate. It's all I can find." I can tell by the whiney voice he's hoping I'll take it. "It'll be OK," I answer. When we get there, it's not OK. The small room has a twin bed, a sink and a metal box, a little bigger than a coffin, that turns out to be the shower. There's no toilet. I have to use the public one on the other side of the registration desk. The old man at the desk smirks, "I can get you a chamber pot if you'd like." Under a thatch of white hair, his is face is as brown and creased as my old leather gloves. His astute blue eyes stare at me without wavering. "Hank" is embroidered on his shirt pocket.

"Look, Hank, I know how to use a restroom. This is like the summer camps I stayed at when I was a kid." I don't tell either my husband or the old geezer how much I hated summer camp.

The first week's not bad. I get familiar with the hiking trails see moose drinking at the lake, black bears loping up a hillside. The Wagon Wheel restaurant serves good, hearty food and after my hikes, I really appreciate it. The gift shop has a large collection of paperbacks and I spend my evenings catching up on Sue Grafton's "alphabet mysteries" series.

During a late afternoon hike I notice a small beach with bathers at the far end of the lake. When I ask Hank about it, he drawls, "There's a hot spring there and all the old hippies come to soak. They're naked as jay birds."

"Oh, that won't bother me," I answer and decide to take a swim tomorrow morning.

I'm there early and when I step into the lake, the water is so cold it curls my toes and tingles my flesh. When I finally find the warm spring, my muscles relax as the mineral-rich water surrounds me. It's as fine as any spa Jacuzzi. No, it's better. The air is pine perfumed, birds are twittering and there's a doe with her fawn lapping water. I float lulled by the warmth and the quiet. I don't notice her until she bleats, "Hi, there. Isn't this the greatest spot?" When I turn, she gasps. "Whatever happened to your face?"

A pudgy, naked woman is walking into the water like Botticelli's aged Venus. "I fell and hit my forehead," I answer. She's making no effort to cover her privates but is busy pinning her grey hair up with a tortoise-shell clip. I'm in water up to my neck, so I slip off the straps of my two-piece bathing suit and lower the top to my waist. There's no way I'll let her think I'm a prude. I'll never see forty again but I'm still in good shape and proud of it. My dark hair needs only an occasional touch-up from the hairdresser. I don't want to chit chat and paddle away but I'm not going to parade myself naked in front of her and plan to stay in the water until she leaves.

Soon I'm as wrinkled as a basset hound and she's still making no effort to go. Finally, she heads toward shore but stops and begins to madly wave her arm shouting, "Jerry! Jerry!" Her under-arm flab jiggles almost as much as her pendulous breasts. A barrel of a man is heading toward us. He drops his towel revealing a watermelon-round belly and a gray nest of hair underneath. The tip of a fat pink worm peeks out of the nest. Neither one of them seems to be the least bit self-conscious. They chat, splash and chortle for hours and I'm stuck without the self-assurance to either pull up my top or to shed my suit and walk out of the water.

After one particularly loud whoop, they amble to shore carelessly draped in their towels; her left buttock peeks out like an under-baked biscuit. I can hardly get to my room fast enough. Hank is behind the registration desk and asks, "How was the swim?"

"Some people around here need to look at a full length mirror," I answer and slam my door.

The second week starts with rain showers and by the middle of the week, it's a continual downpour. The trails are slick clay and hikes are impossible. Without rain gear, I'm drenched before I get to the restaurant for meals. Hank had offered to drive me but I snapped at him, "It's only a few hundred feet." He hasn't offered again. By Thursday night, I'm going nuts in my small room. There's a timid knock on my door and I find Hank standing there. "Do you know how to play euchre?" he asks.

"Euchre? Yeah, I do." I remember summer nights with Uncle Studie and Aunt Em playing euchre while blackberry pies cooled on the kitchen counter. "Well, come on," he says. We run across to his cabin and he has a card table set up with two piles of pennies for our stakes. It's a tricky game and it's been a long time since I've played so I lose consistently but don't mind. Hank helps me out, gives me pointers and it doesn't seem like a contest between us.

We take a break from the card game and Hank brings out two steaming mugs of coffee. "You've seen Yellowstone haven't you?" He asks.

I decide to tell him the truth. "Yeah and I hated it, all the steam, geysers and vapors, the earth shifting and liquid. It just seems wrong somehow. I'm from the Midwest and I like the ground to be solid under my feet, not churning and bubbling."

"Well, I never thought like that." Hank says. "I ran off from our farm in Indiana when I was 16 after a big fight with my pa. When I got to this place, I knew it was where I wanted to stay. I love this land. It's alive, always changing, being reborn. If the earth could have such new life, I felt I could, too." He begins to deal our cards. We don't talk much the rest of the evening.

At breakfast I ask my waitress to wrap two pecan rolls, hoping we play euchre again tonight. The rain has let up a little but I spend the day in my room thinking about Paul, about our life. As I head out to dinner I see Hank.

"Are we playing euchre tonight?" I ask.

"Sure, if you want. Come on over around seven."

I'm on time and hand him the bag with the pecan rolls. After a few games, we sip coffee and nibble the rolls. Since he's spoken about himself the night before, I want to confide in him. Sometimes it's more comfortable to tell your secrets to strangers, people on a train or plane, people you'll never see again.

"I got this bruise when I fell and hit the corner of a cocktail table, but I let people think that Paul was responsible." Hank is poker faced and I stammer as I try to justify myself. "Paul is so controlling, so...self-centered. It may seem unfair...he nags and harangues me...I manipulate him...oh, I just can't explain what it's like to live with him."

The only sound is the card slapping on the table. After a while Hank clears his throat. "Early this summer there was a bear that came down to the buildings here. Tourists threw food to him and, even though the rangers moved him to the wilderness a couple of times, he kept coming back. They finally had to put him down."

The story seems pointless to me. "What's that about?" I ask. "Is it about Paul and me?" There's a long silence before Hank answers.

"I recon' what I'm saying is the bear acted like a bear and the tourists acted like tourists but they are the ones who are aware of their actions. They wanted to see the bear up close and didn't think about what feeding him meant in the great scheme of things."

I plead a headache and end the game early. The weather has cleared and, before returning to my room, I gaze at the clusters of stars in the sky. I'd like to call Paul and ask him if his skies are clear, but cell phones don't work here. We haven't talked for two weeks and I haven't missed him. Is he's happier without me? Why have we stayed together? I can only prod at my motivations. I know he's book wise and life foolish, that our time together is one long contest. I'm pleased when I get the better of him and he's always looking to improve me. Is this how I want to live? Can I live apart from him?

In the Spring
Nancy J. Sparks

They are highly prized by French cuisine, sell for upwards of $50 a pound, and create a frenzy among hunters whenever they are found. They have websites, Facebook pages, and texts fly back and forth among hunters tracking their appearances. They come in black, yellow and grey, as well as other colors and are found throughout most of the U.S. Are they an exotic type of game running through the forest, evading hunters to preserve the species? No. It is the lowly morel mushroom. And they are absolutely, positively, delicious.

Morels have been a part of my life since I was a child. Though the arrival of spring means many things to people who drag out their barbeques on the first nice day or run to the beach in short shorts to shiver as they lay on towels in the sand, spring means just one thing to me— mushrooms. My father started mushroom hunting in the hills of Lafayette, Indiana when he was a boy. It was during the Depression, and he and his five brothers did what they could to contribute to the family's food supply. When a relative told the tow-headed boys that they could eat the odd-looking fungus that grew wild in the spring woods, they hunted tirelessly, bringing bagfuls home to their widowed mother. At dinner they gathered around the solid oak dining table, anxious to slap the butter-fried bites onto homemade white bread, filling their stomachs for the night.

My dad carried the mushroom hunting tradition into his adult years, as did his brothers. Every year when I was young we would all gather in those same hills on warm spring weekends and hunt the elusive mushroom. Everyone carried paper grocery sacks and tromped through wooded areas, with "Got one!" ringing through the air when someone was lucky enough to stumble across a specimen. As a child it was frustrating to me to be forced to go along on these weekends, when I'd much rather be home watching Saturday morning cartoons. Josie and the Pussycats, Scooby Doo and the Bugs Bunny/Roadrunner Hour were much more appealing than a little brown thing that popped up out of the dirt. Most of the time I would lay in the back seat of my parent's Chrysler New Yorker, with books by my side providing my escape. While my relatives foraged in the warm woods I would lose myself in the Hardy Boys books (Nancy Drew was too prissy for me), shivering as I explored a haunted mansion with Joe and Frank Hardy. Books aside, these trips were the ultimate of boredom for me, but I must admit when my mom brought our morels home and fried them in butter...the taste was heavenly.

Friends at school thought my family was crazy. Wild mushrooms were poisonous! Even my science teacher warned me with all seriousness about fake morels that would kill me before the tiny bite had cleared my tongue. I tried to pass these warnings on to my parents, but would always get a sigh and the response. "We know what we're doing." Once I ventured into the school library and looked up the poisonous imposter in the cherished World Book Encyclopedia, and was unable to distinguish it from its safe counterpart. I passed on the mushrooms that year. Miraculously, none of my family died.

The next year I was back on the hunt. Something about finding the wrinkled, sponge looking fungi became a personal challenge. I gave up the cartoons and books, and would go out on my own, scouring the woods behind our house. We could never find enough for a feast, so each tiny mushroom was treated like gold and doled out as such. Some years had abundant yields, some had little. It all depended on the timing of sun and rain. One year when days of hunting had produced very few morels, my Uncle Lawrence and Aunt Mae drove up into Michigan to a morel festival, where they purchased 10 pounds of the tasty things. The entire family gathered at their home the next weekend. The men stood in the yard around Lawrence's new mower, talking about its pros and cons. The women, who were banned from the kitchen, sat on the patio sipping tea, throwing nervous glances at the door. My Aunt Mae loved to boast about her cooking, but her culinary skills were dubious at best. When she came to the door in her "World's Best Cook" apron, her silver hair in disarray and her face beet red, my mom's brown eyes grew even darker and she muttered, "Mark my words, she's ruined them!" Everyone rushed into the dining room and watched in anticipation as Aunt Mae brought a tray out of the kitchen with two large bowls of...a brown gooey-looking substance. Instead of the tantalizing scent of butter, the smell of black pepper permeated the air. My uncle followed with plates of white bread. "TA-DAH," Aunt Mae crowed with her smoker's voice as she placed the bowls on the table with fanfare, one at each end. My aunts and uncles looked at each other, and the bravest aunt wrinkled her nose and asked "What did you do to them?"

Aunt Mae pulled her stocky frame as tall as she could and proclaimed, "I made creamed mushrooms! It's my own recipe! Dig in!" With some trepidation, everyone helped themselves and looks of anticipation turned to grimaces. The morels were chopped up so small they were almost unidentifiable, and the black pepper overpowered the entire dish. I'll give the relatives credit though; everyone managed to choke some down except me. I couldn't stand pepper, so I slipped from the table while everyone was having polite conversation and went to the bathroom and washed my tongue to try to stop the burning. Needless to say, our yearning for morels went unfulfilled that year.

:✹●: :✹●: :✹●:

From his childhood beginnings to his death, my dad always took his search for morels seriously. When the grass was just getting high enough for mowing he would start scouring our yard, looking under piles of leftover winter leaves and downed branches. I would watch out the kitchen window and see his lanky frame wandering through the trees, his blond hair fluttering around his face. He would proudly bring the first mushroom inside and present it to my mom, his blue eyes shining. Beaming her large smile that showed her dimples and the tiny lines just beginning to form around her eyes, she'd give him a kiss, and ceremoniously place it in a bowl of cold water in the fridge and he would go out searching for more. He would mark his finds with a stick, letting them grow additional days, hoping no bird or squirrel would raid his treasure. At the peak of their growth, he would pick the mushrooms and we would gather in the kitchen as my mom sliced them carefully. After they were fried she carefully divided them between us so we each got an equal taste.

:✹●: :✹●: :✹●:

The year my mom died, he found only one, and presented it to me with trembling, wrinkled hands. I gave him a peck on the cheek, and placed the morel it in its bowl of cold water in the fridge. He stumbled around the yard lost and alone, his faded blue eyes looking but not seeing. The mushroom sat in the fridge until it withered and I eventually threw it away. The next year he searched the yard stooped over his cane. The year after, he dragged himself around with a walker. No morels appeared. They had moved on. He never gave up hope, and always mustered up the strength to go out and search in the spring. He died in the spring of 2009, a month before mushroom season began.

That April I was cleaning out his things, and after a particularly hard day I decided to take a break. The spring sun felt warm on my shoulders as I walked through the yard. I sat down by an old, dead cottonwood, and watched the robins hop around the grass, searching for lunch. I looked down, and there by my hand, was a morel. I looked around and there was another, and another and another! I called to my husband and daughter, who were still sorting through things, grabbed some bags, and by the time we were finished we had picked 192 morels, by far the most we had ever found. We brought them in the house and poured bagful after bagful on the kitchen table, staring in amazement. They watched as I cleaned, sliced and fried the morels, and then served huge platefuls. We relished each bite, wishing my dad could have been there for the feast.

Now I am the one who scours the yard. Some days my daughter joins me in, her blond head visible as she pokes through the dead leaves, the sun warm on our shoulders as spring begins again.

After Lights Was Out
Carla Stout

The sky is gray as liver and onions
in a cast iron pan while I roll up
my mattress fast as can be. They say

it'll sleet today topping off eight inches
of heavy snow in what my buddy, Leo,
slept so late he never woke up. I don't know

where they laid him but I'm goddam sure
it were the cold that killed him. Long after
lights was out, I played him the only song I

knowed, "Plastic Jesus," on the harmonica
and they was all buzzing 'bout Leo in the library,
not listening to a word I say, "By God, the birds is back

today." You can send your sorrows to the bus
stop at Thirteenth and State where me and Leo
live in cardboard boxes warped with ice, where buses

will splash you but they ain't never late. Windows
at the library is all steamed up. Guess it's all
that heavy breathing over Dante, Shakespeare

and National Geographic, Leo's favorite, like
his size twelve rubber boots I make fit
with crumpled newspaper. It's sleeting now,
but hell, Leo, by God, the birds is back.

Central Illinois, Late October

Judith Valente

The season spills out its fistful of playing marbles:
    millefiores, sunbursts, oxbloods, caneswirls.

Bronze leaves hang,
    their gnarled hands empty of pennies. Death smell hangs,
    moist fomenting cider in the tight-chested ground.

I steady myself for the cardboard colors to come:
    Dun, amber and sepia seeping across ungrazed prairie.

Saturday. The afternoon drive past
    Dwight-Odell- Pontiac- Towanda

Familiar markers rise
    like roadside crosses for the dead:
  Sun Motel- Pete's Harvest Table- Robert Bolen Stock Farms

Whether castle, hut or geodesic dome
    Guns save lives in our homes:

the words take root like old Burma Shave ads beside cross-stitches
    of corn, soybean soon to dissolve, absolve
    in a font of 5 p.m. cobalt blue.

Spring is an O of astonishment.
    This, this is the pursed lip of a B. Mouth slammed
    shut on the tongue. Steel casing snapped
    in place over a coffin

    as we dangle between eternity
    and the dry, uncertain landscape,
tabula rasa and our own imperfect and wavering perspective.

Romantics Would Walk Cleanly into December
Claudia Van Gerven

Romantics would walk cleanly into December
into the clean story of
winter, classic, remorseless
where even trees are
spare and upright

but for this lush light of October
when locust lilts frill upon frill
of yellow breeze and we hesitate in up-rush
of scarlet, of vermilion, are caught
in excrescences of leaves, the grasp of
wild grasses that cling to ankles, to knees

so that we forget
the austere plot
the hero dead
the stripped maple that climbs
concisely into night
to wallow in the richness of leave-taking
the thousand yellow pities, these urgent
superfluous good-byes.

The Fallen
Claudia Van Gerven

Saint Francis stands resolutely atop the trapdoor
to corruption,

feeding miscellaneous birds with his bowl of seeds.
A procession of spongy acolytes, white hooded, heads bowed,

march steadily from beneath his terra cote robes
across a plinth of stump.

The cottonwood felled so long ago still sends these pilgrims,
boneless and silent, walking the old roots.

Across the fence, a living sprout, green-faced,
luminous, beams at these

other resurrections with their delicate,
crepey bellies of hopeful poisons.

Life is strolling
across graves, across property lines.

What can Death mean—
or Spring?

The Ultimate Power of No

Dianalee Velie

Eighteen months old, running, rarely walking,
my grandson repeats his favorite word
five times over again, a litany
of new negative possibilities:
no, no, no, no, no.

A diaper changed while watching Jungle Book,
his favorite movie? Lunch this afternoon
when he doesn't feel like eating today?
He relishes his ultimate power:
no, no, no, no, no.

Like a morning glory opening up
to the daylight, he is focused, secure,
receptive to each new day of freedoms,
while, miles away, his great-grandfather
refuses all food and medications.

No, no, no, no, no,
he reiterates to care givers who
try to coax spoonfuls of water or broth
through thin parched lips or move him in bed,
his life's path scrolling up now behind him.

No, no, no, no no,
he is focused and secure, ready to close
like a morning glory in the gentle night.
Changes, occurring in the changeless,
driven by the ultimate power of no.

The Baobab Seed

Anthony R. White

I am the green life inside the nut,
so folded you would think I'm old.
But I am before young. I wait in the before-time,
dream leafy canopies high above the veldt.
Breezes. Rain. Star blaze.
My only hope: That a hungry elephant
will pass this way
and swallow me.

I'm no ostrich—I have no egg-tooth
to chisel my way out of this hard black shell.
But if that great gray sniffer sniffs me out,
lifts me past the two ivory gatekeepers,
into the steaming wet tunnel—ah,
then the raging tide of digestion, that acid hurricane,
may be enough to soften my outer hull,
this black lifeboat I ride.

Nothing moves from here to the horizon.
A cheetah coughs in the branches overhead.
Plenty of time.

The Way of the Kami: A Shinto Zen Buddhist Rock Garden
Martin Willitts, Jr.

There is beauty in each stone. One stone
is white as a crane. An almond stone is the color
of my wife's eyes. I do not count each stone.
Each stone must be placed exactly where it belongs.
It must not be disturbed. Notice the tone and voice
of each pebble no matter how small. Listen carefully
as it tells you about our ancestors. It will tell you
how it used to be a mountain.

A sandalwood stick burns to purify the garden.
It pleases the Kami. I will not have any bad dreams tonight.
My wife will giggle in my arms as we discover each other
like the first time. This is the result of such careful gardening.
Her voice sings in each pebble.

I am careful while sweeping the rocks so as to not disrupt their rest.
I can almost smell fish cooked in wrapped seaweed
and served with jasmine tea as I rake sand. It surrounds the reflecting pool
with Koi shimmering like the sun. It swims my wife's name
as the sand is brushed like her hair. Everything ripples,
even the air.

Her laughter climbs the garden walls into the sky.
It dances with our ancestors.
The night swirls like tea.

Even the broom smiles.

Winter's Wind

Karin Wisiol

Second cup of coffee: through thermopane I watch
men nail roof tiles, no rope, knit caps down to their eyes.

After noon I check the horses in their hill paddocks.
They hunch, head down, bulky in polyfill blankets.

Inside the stable, oldsters toss and re-toss hay.
They flick an ear at my voice and fidget, cranky.

Outside, four bluebirds a month early for north Illinois
sway on a cedar. Barn-cat grins: "I'll see they don't suffer."

Near midnight, clear from the farm hedgerow, an owl's
who-who-whoo enters my window, open only an inch.

Bedtime reading: of the long-aproned plains women
struck full-body by wind sickness, some went dumb mid-

sentence. Some, un-smiling ever, counted their steps
in the ruts as they trekked back east. A few were carried.

Changing Gears
Paula Yup

I stroll by placing foot before foot
because the Indian cotton dress I wear
of lavender and green flowers against white
only allows small steps.

I am this day a lady. It is so still and quiet
that the trees seem to rustle like dresses
of fine young ladies.
In thoughts I can paint with ease
lines and lines of a nude descending winding stairs.

Los Angeles, that angel's freeway, is far away.
My friends there drive fast lives. Their analysts lay them flat
and iron them pretty as *Vogue* covergirls.
They were the rich oil of an exotic sauce
and I was the poor water of my own tears.
Now I post myself civil with little notes.

I am slow, prefer the trees for conversation
and my books for company. Ponds are my eyes.
Ships are my ears.
Foghorns blow me away to Martha's Vineyard
in my sleep. My arm curls about my love's waist
and I am slow and sleepy in the deep.

Winter Came
Peggy Zabicki

The soggy leaves on the forsythia bush
Didn't have time to turn orange
And crunchy
Before the snow came.
So, there they hang
Heavy and wet
Where there should only be bare branches
And twigs
With a light sprinkle of snowflakes.
No one minds that.
No one sad that autumn is over
Except me
Because the leaves are still
On the bushes
And they remind me
In a heavy and wet way
Of all the things I didn't do
Before winter came.

The Things We Can Change...

Those who have lost loved ones to drunk drivers know
how quickly a whole world can change...

We can work together to ensure such loss will not
happen again.

In memoriam

Stephen George Hough

May 24, 1981 - April 29, 2008

One moment Bonnie Hough was in her garden, a proud mom anticipating her son's graduation from Purdue University—just 10 days away. A moment later, twice-convicted drunk driver Mario Cadena, whose blood-alcohol concentration was more than double Indiana's legal limit, drove at 85 miles per hour on the wrong side of the road through a stop sign, causing a three-car crash which killed Ronald and Bonnie's son Stephen, 26, and his fiancee, Amy Bartelmey, 25.

"Nothing can prepare you," Bonnie says, recalling the police knocking at her door and notifying her of the dreadful loss. The news headline: Four Killed in 3 Car Accident, "can't capture our shock and loss; our grief when we took our only son's diploma to the cemetery where we'd buried him four days prior."

Compassionate, loving and hardworking, public relations graduate Stephen was an expert skier and avid Chicago Bears fan who enjoyed going skiing and to Bears games with their dad, recalls his sister, Lauren Heart. "I was always in awe of my big brother," she says. "His protection, friendship and advice have helped me throughout my life. He was going to adopt Amy's little boy, Gauje, and they wanted two more kids. Steve would have been a great dad."

"We will never hold their babies. Our children and future grandchildren are already lost to us," says Bonnie. "Amy wanted to be cremated and Steve to be buried. We placed Amy's urn in Stephen's arms and buried them together." Ron says, "The headstone reads, 'Step softly. Our dreams lie buried here.'"

Here is a glimpse of a life that could have been; a life cut tragically short. It gives us a sense of an unlived future as a husband to Amy and a dad to Gauje. "Remember Steve not just as an accident statistic or a promising young man, but as a vibrant symbol of change to rid our roads of drunk drivers," Bonnie urges as she takes solace in a comforting poem.

The Broken Chain

Ron Tranmer

We little knew that day,
God was going to call your name.
In life we loved you dearly,
in death we do the same.

It broke our hearts to lose you.
You did not go alone.
For part of us went with you,
the day God called you home.

You left us beautiful memories,
your love is till our guide.
And although we cannot see you,
you are always at our side.

Our family chain is broken,
and nothing seems the same,
but as God calls us one by one,
the chain will link again.

"We channel our grief by advocating for the use of court-ordered ignition interlock systems," says Ron. These systems require periodic breath tests for drivers, not only when starting the vehicle but randomly through the course of the drive. He adds, "If a driver fails to blow when the device requires it, the car will shut itself off. Let's join forces to end these needless, preventable deaths."

≋≋≋ ≋≋≋ ≋≋≋

Visit the Mothers Against Drunk Drivers site, www.madd.org, and click on "Take Action" to contact your representatives; help make alcohol ignition interlocks mandatory for all convicted drunk drivers.

Purdue University-Calumet has started the Steve Hough Memorial Scholarship for the most promising public relations students. To contribute, send a check payable to the Stephen Hough Memorial Scholarship to Purdue's Office of Advancement, 2200 169th Street, Hammond, IN 46323

Stanton Richard Segner
June 19, 1966 - May 2, 1997

Life and Death of an Artist: one of the most promising young artists in Denver's art community, Stan Segner, owner of the Segner SteelWorks Gallery, was killed when the car in which he was a passenger was struck by another vehicle driven by a drunk driver who'd literally been drinking all day. Stan was just beginning to see some recognition of his talent following years of being "a struggling young artist" devoting himself to creating unusual sculptures from steel and chrome car bumpers–"junk art" from furniture to oversized motorcycled to enormous metal heads. He typified the school of fierce, in-your-face creativity.

"He could plasma cut and arc weld metals so that they magically became beautiful works of art and furniture," says his father, Fred Segner. "Stan loved football, disk golf, motorcycles, beer, pretty girls, and dogs. He hated textbooks, phony people, and what he called the 'paper crap' associated with being a businessman."

As a boy Stan's formidable eye/body coordination made him an outstanding middle linebacker and helped develop skills he would use as an artist. "He could diagnose and destroy an opponent's football play. Just as easily he could cause an art or political concept to flow from an idea in his mind, through his powerful arms and hands, into artistic reality," Fred says.

The Stanton Segner Memorial Foundation enriches public school arts programming by providing speakers and materials as well as making possible the annual Stanton Segner Award. For details see www.segner.com.

Pat, Stan's mom, recalls their son as an active baby and toddler with dark, curly hair and bright blue eyes. He had a daredevil quality and jumped into the deep end of a motel swimming pool when he was three years old. "Dad made a fast rescue," she says. "In school my son liked creative projects and challenges, was charming and generous to his friends, and liked to pull pranks."

She continues, "Often I think of how easy and joyous it was to give birth to Stan, who was born, the largest of my babies at 7 pounds, 8 ounces in four hours of natural childbirth–this birth in stark contrast to his horrible, unnecessary death at the hands of a drunk driver." The Segners have some of their son's work in their house and yard where Stan's oversized angels stand watch over his whimsical furniture and his dad's garden. Says Pat, "Stan's sculptures, some of them in my home, are a way he lives on, but that he can no longer contribute creative ideas seems a monstrous waste."

Two Poems for Stan by Bev Dudey

Walking Along

We are walking along
and then there is nothing

There is being
There is nothing

We all know this
We never know this

Be still and know

Once there is being
There is never nothing

We must touch hands
and keep walking along

Look to See

Look to see
the gleam of angel wings
dancing in the grass

Pause to feel
the wind blowing
a motorcycle along

Stop and sense
the glimmer of
an ancient circle

Know this to be

IMMORTALITY

About TallGrass Writers Guild

TallGrass Writers Guild is open to all who write seriously at any level. The Guild supports members by providing performance and publication opportunities via its multi-page, bi-monthly newsletter, open mics, formal readings, annual anthologies, and the TallGrass Writers Guild Performance Ensemble programs. In affiliation with Outrider Press, TallGrass produces its annual "Black-and-White" anthologies, the results of international calls for themed contest entries. Cash prizes and certificates awarded result from the decisions of independent judges. The Guild is a rarity among arts organizations in that it has been and remains largely self-sufficient despite the challenges facing non-profit arts organizations. For more information on TallGrass Writers Guild membership and programs, call 219-322-7270 or toll-free at 1-866-510-6735. Email tallgrassguild@sbcglobal.net .

About the Judge

Diane ("Diva Di") Williams, author of *Performing Seals*, is a prize-winning poet and essayist who has a novel in progress. A graduate of Chicago's Columbia College, "Judge Diva" was awarded a literary fellowship that took her to Ireland for extensive study. She lives and writes in Chicago, and teaches at Kendall College.

About the Editor

Whitney Scott plays many roles in Chicago's literary scene. She is an author, editor, book designer and reviewer whose poetry, fiction and creative nonfiction have been published internationally, earning her listings in *Contemporary Authors* and *Directory of American Poets and Fiction Writers*. A member of the Society of Midland Authors, she performs her work at colleges, universities, arts festivals and literary venues throughout the Chicago area and has been featured as guest author in the Illinois Authors Series at Chicago's Harold Washington Library. Scott was awarded the 2009-10 Writer-in-Residence Award from Bensenville Public Library, is judge of the 2010 National Federation of Press Women writing competition, and regularly reviews books for the American Library Association's *Booklist* magazine.

To Order
Outrider Press Publications
effective January 1 2000, all prices include applicable taxes

_____ **Seasons of Change** –$21.00

Writings on the natural world, technology, personal identity...   _____

_____ **Fearsome Fascinations** –$21.00

Writings on bad boys, vamps, werewolves, forbidden fruits of all kind   _____

_____ **Wild Things — Domestic & Otherwise** –$21.00

Writings on bats, rivers...children running wild...   _____

_____ **A Walk Through My Garden**–$21.00

Writings on crocuses, composting, digital gardens and more   _____

_____ **Vacations: the Good, the Bad & the Ugly** – $20.00

Writings on respites from stolen moments to Roman holidays   _____

_____ **Falling in Love Again** – $20.00

Writings on revisiting romance, beloved locales and more   _____

_____ **Family Gatherings** – $20.00

Writings on families   _____

_____ **Take Two — They're Small** – $20.00

Writings on food   _____

_____ **A Kiss Is Still A Kiss** – $19.00

Writings on romantic love   _____

_____ **Earth Beneath, Sky Beyond** – $19.00

An anthology on nature and our planet   _____

_____ **Feathers, Fins & Fur** – $18.00

Writings on animals   _____

_____ **Freedom's Just Another Word** – $17.00

Poetry, fiction and essay on freedom   _____

_____ **Alternatives: Roads Less Travelled** – $17.00

Writings on counter-culture lifestyles   _____

_____ **Prairie Hearts** – $17.00

Short fiction and poetry on the Heartland   _____

_____ **Dancing** to the End of the **Shining Bar** – $11.95

A novel of love and courage   _____

Add s/h charges:
$3.95 for 1 book...$6.95 for 2 books...
$2.25 each additional book   ▬▬▬▬▬▬

Send Check or $ Order to:
Outrider Press, Inc.
2036 North Winds Drive   Total _____
Dyer, IN 46311